Contents

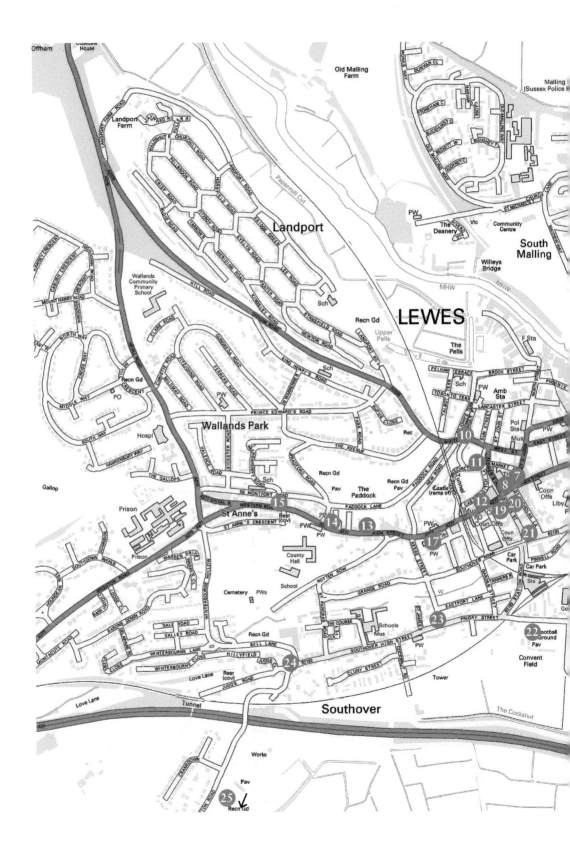

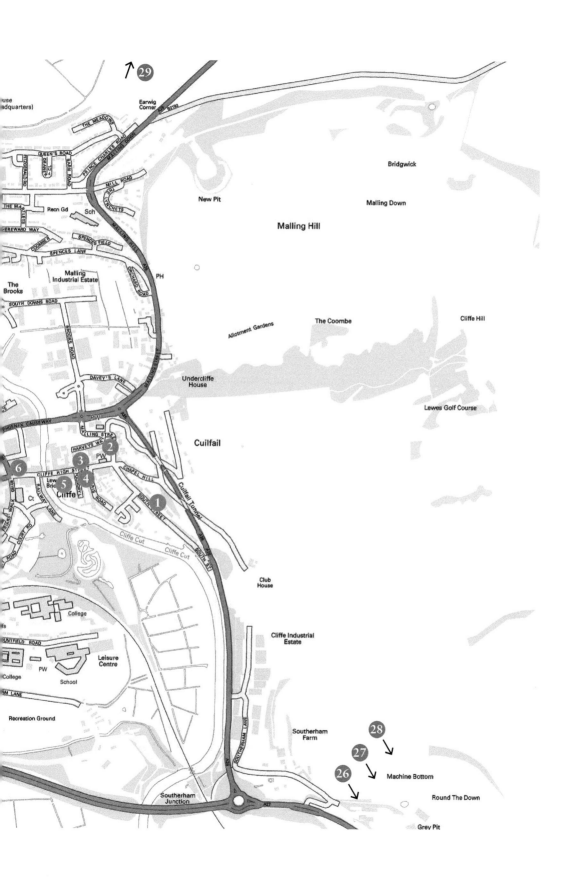

List of Pubs

1. The Snowdrop Inn, South Street, Cliffe
2. The Dorset, Malling Street
3. The Real Eating Company, Cliffe High Street
4. The Gardener's Arms, Cliffe High Street
5. The John Harvey Tavern, Bear Lane, off Cliffe High Street
6. The Volunteer, Eastgate Street
7. The Crown Hotel, Market Street/School Hill
8. The Star, High Street
9. The Lamb, Fisher Street
10. The Elephant & Castle, White Hill
11. The Lewes Arms, Castle Precincts
12. The Rights of Man, High Street
13. The Shelleys, High Street
14. The Pelham Arms, St Anne's Hill
15. The Black Horse, Western Road
16. The Tally Ho, Baxter Road, Landport
17. The Brewers Arms, High Street
18. The Pelham House Hotel, St Andrew's Lane
19. The White Hart, High Street
20. The Royal Oak, Station Street
21. Lansdown Arms, Station Street
22. The Rooks Inn, Southover
23. The King's Head, Southover
24. The Swan Inn, Southover High Street
25. The Juggs, Wellgreen Lane, Kingston
26. The Ram Inn, Firle
27. The Cricketers, Berwick Village (off A27 to Eastbourne)
28. The Trevor, Glynde
29. The Anchor Inn, Barcombe

Introduction

In 2004, John Eccles, chief reporter of the Lewes-based *Sussex Express* newspaper, when quoted in David Arscott's excellent *Our Lewes* book, subjected the author to a minor telling-off: 'You're organising the book by areas,' he said, 'I'd have done it by pubs. There are so many and they each have their own character.'

Hopefully here in *Lewes Pubs* we're doing both. This book attempts to tell the story of Lewes' pubs today and in the past, painting a picture of this fantastic hillside, riverside and cliffside town, which (for the unaware) is really separated by the River Ouse into two settlements, Lewes and (the) Cliffe, each with an historic but friendly rivalry. Therefore, we have taken the Ouse as the first divide to split up the book by area, starting with the pubs east of the river in Cliffe, before travelling up the main street westwards to explore the pubs north and then south of the High Street of Lewes itself. We then move to Southover before finally heading out of the town. Some may ask why would anyone want to leave Lewes, and this is true in part; the town has endless charms for both resident and visitor but is also in a charming environment, with the beautiful Ouse valley, South Downs, Chapel Hill and country lanes leading you away for interesting drives or wonderful walks. This then, is where the book goes too.

For those wanting to experience more pubs than a rugby team has players we need to journey to the wonderful villages such as Kingston, Firle and Glynde. However, a rural walk is always the best way to reach a pub and there is no better way to work up a thirst. John Eccles is correct in that for a town of its size, Lewes does punch above its weight in terms of the number of pubs it still has, serving all areas of the community,

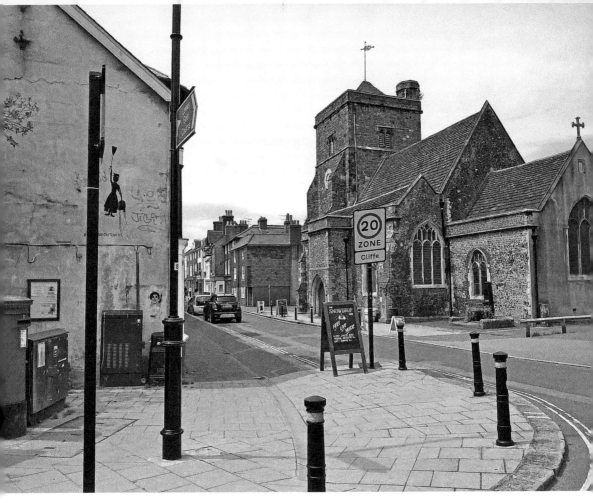

Cliffe High Street: the site of many more pubs until the early twentieth century.

propped up by the town's many visitors, tourists, incoming commuter population as well as a lively bunch of academics, students and the sociable, many of whom are used to the frenetic pub scene in Brighton.

I have spent a large amount of time in Lewes as a Sussex bloke myself, unfortunately mostly as a teacher leading hundreds of children around the town on history trips, so it wasn't really the perfect opportunity to enjoy a quiet pint. Much as I tried. According to risk assessments, apparently you just can't leave thirty-five Year 7s outside by a busy road while you have a nice pint of Hophead. It is my first choice though today for days out with my own children and, to finally get that aforementioned quiet pint (or two), I come with friends and family whenever the opportunity arises. There are few more interesting places in the country for mooching for antiques and books, walks, beautiful views and, of course, exploring decent pubs.

For a young boy growing up in Brighton, Lewes was always far more exciting. Admittedly, Brighton may have had a palace but Lewes had a *castle*. A proper one as well. The Pavilion may have had a king in it, whereas Lewes Castle only had a king's mate in it, but George IV seemed a bit of a ponce – but Lewes had knights and fighting and death and blood and battles. The palace was for George to do lots of snogging, whereas Lewes had swords, stabbing and squirting blood by the gallon. No contest. Today I still can't walk around Lewes' wonderful layout without being an eight-year-old imagining the spooky twittens, masses of monks, blood spilling on the hills above and King Alfred's men constructing the walls of the town in its time as a *burh*, a military fort in the late 800s. I also love the fact that as you walk around the unusual layout of Lewes you discover the tales of not just kings and knights, but ordinary folk too. I love the way that Lewes pub and brewery ownership has been passed down from generation to generation, of the charismatic landladies that ran and still run the town's taverns and the stories of the ordinary farmers, factory workers, smugglers and soldiers that frequented them.

The layout of Lewes (pronounced 'Loo-ez', although you might get away with 'Loo-es', but never 'Loos' as some metropolitan travel reporters still pronounce it) is key to its charm for pub-goers. As a mostly linear settlement – its High Street is an earlier route of the busy Sussex west–east A27 Honiton–Folkestone trunk road – it has no town centre as such. The only place that could technically be its geographical heart, in the area outside the Town Hall, has only one pub, the Crown Inn. The Crown, although an imposing and gorgeous Georgian building with the friendliest of regulars is not in the best state of repair. This centre of Lewes, if we are to call it that, is also not the most ideal of urban spaces, as a busy traffic corner was once Tudor Sussex's equivalent of Tiananmen Square, the site of the mass murder of seventeen Protestant martyrs. The upside to this is that there is no preponderance of pubs in any particular area what with Lewes having no town centre as such; no village green equivalent that you don't want to leave. So this means that Lewes presents a decent (and downhill) descending trail for the serious pub-crawler heading east, but anyone so doing will miss the delights of Southover's taverns, of the Snowdrop and of cosy and intimate pubs such as the Lewes Arms, or valued local boozers such as the Black Horse and the Tally Ho. Finding Lewes' pubs in a meandering, haphazard fashion makes a far more interesting method of exploring and getting to know this beautiful and historic county town.

Of course, I would never recommend that anyone attempts all the central Lewes pubs and venues in this book in one go, rather it is a guide to a pub crawl over a series of several very pleasant days. The outer pubs I mention in the last chapter should of course involve one or more separate, good walks or the use of a designated driver. The only two that are of reasonable walking distance with each other are the Ram and the Trevor – and here I would urge caution crossing that busy but narrow Sussex artery that is the A27.

However, I do also recommend that people get out and use, support and enjoy our pubs, whether their local or trying new or revamped venues. In these days of increasing solo accommodation, loneliness in old age and where tearing ourselves away from screens of all sizes is becoming rarer, having places to meet, discuss, laugh and make face-to-face contact should become cherished as the important respite from mobile phones and plasma screens. Humans have gathered in meeting places since at least the Stone Age. Pubs are needed more now than ever. Whether you are an imbiber of alcohol, a diner or just a coffee-quaffer, places to gather are just as important as they were millennia ago as we make our way through, what Greg Jenner, one of the writers of *Horrible Histories*, calls the 'Phone Age'. I hope that the most settled of regular will use this book as a chance to see what regulars in other pubs are being offered and explore perhaps one new pub they haven't ventured into for years. I will be a very happy author if the book encourages not only more visitors to Lewes to explore the venues that very lucky Lewesians have at their doorstep, but that citizens of the town itself try other pubs that they haven't visited before or for years. Lewesians are indeed fortunate: not only do they have an exciting, historic and beautiful town but they have pubs like the Elly, Brewers, Snowdrop and the Crown where you actually experience something quite rare these days – a genuine *welcome* and a feeling of community where you are welcomed in to someone else's 'family'. Surely this must be the Holy Grail that all pub owners and landlords seek, that mark of excellence – a public house where you don't just feel like a member of the public?

The Home of Harveys
Lewes is all the more special as a town of great English pubs because it is still a town that has not only enjoyed the craft beer revolution of recent

years, but is also a traditional and much-lauded town of traditional brewing, and has been throughout its history. Lewes once had nine breweries (and famously only seven churches) and though today the wider Lewes area also has twenty-two microbreweries, the town itself still has the amazing Harveys brewery, which is not only a well-known symbol of Lewes' and Sussex's most famous beer but is often the expected default beer in Sussex pubs. There have even been protests when Lewes pubs dared stop stocking the one-time county town's champion ale. It is indeed a champion ale: in 2005 and 2006 Harveys Best won the Best Bitter category at the CAMRA's Great British Beer Festival. It has recently been crowned champion in the Tourism Enterprise category of the Countryside Alliance Awards, held at the House of Lords in April 2016. Countryside Alliance Chief Executive Tim Bonner championed the brewery at the awards by saying, 'Harveys Brewery is revered as a Sussex name and embodies all the high standards and values of a bygone era with the seventh and eighth generations of Harvey family at the helm. Trading since 1790, it is the current generation's challenge to merge the old and the new, and this it does to great effect.'

Harveys is also special as brewery tours are conducted personally by the directors, late-night shopping festivals are held in the yard and, quite wonderfully, the company has decided to let its dray horses ride through the town every week for no other reason than that they put a smile on people's faces. Harveys are very proud of their British credentials: all hops are grown within 50 miles, all malt within 90 miles and all by-products are returned to local agriculture, including Plumpton Agricultural College which converts the spent grains into a million pints of milk. 90 per cent of their beer is consumed within 50 miles and the spring water for brewing is drawn via an artesian well 60 feet below their premises. Nor do they add 'booze miles' to the planet's problems – Brighton is as far south as their barrels travel and Harveys refuse to let theirs cross the Thames.

Harveys may today be the last major brewery in the town – after the closures of Beard's, Monks Bear Yard Brewery, South Malling Steam Brewery and Hillman's Southdown Brewery in Cliffe alone – but it is a survivor. It is one of the oldest breweries in the country, having brewed since 1790, and thankfully escaped being taken over by bigger brewery chains in the twentieth century as it never grew too big. It is, amazingly, still in the hands of the same family, seven generations of brewers later.

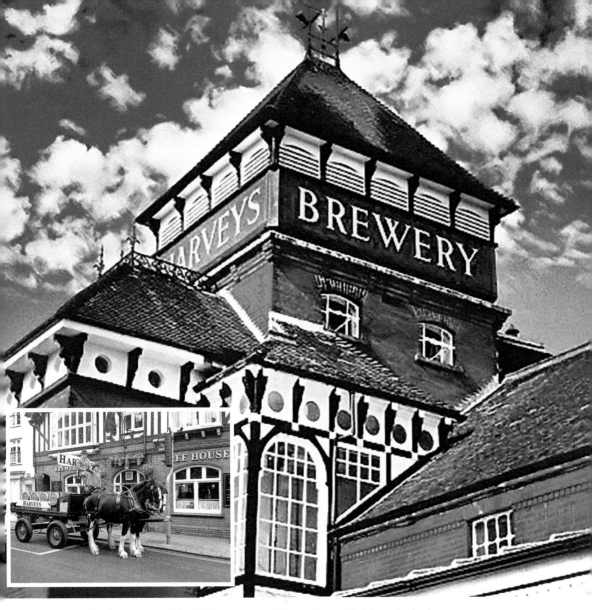

Harveys Brewery, pride of the town and Lewes' unofficial cathedral.
Inset: Harveys' dray horses. (Photo by Paul Dearing, courtesy of www.lewes.co.uk)

One of the other joint directors is Miles Jenner, chief brewer and son of the man credited with saving the brewery, Antony Jenner. Miles' son Edmund has followed his father into the brewing business at Harveys too.

Harveys and its early contemporaries were needed as the town until the mid-twentieth century had its fair share of industry. Manufacturing played a part in the wealth of this Sussex town, although it was more trade and commerce as a market town that made Lewes' economy boom up to the twentieth century. Remarkably, for a small town 7 miles from the coast, Lewes boasted shipbuilding in the 1800s as well as printers, farmers and railway workers. Until recent times, of course, when milk stopped being dangerous and water potentially lethal, beer was far more widely drunk as it was the safest form of liquid.

As well as work, there was play and Lewes' world-renowned bonfire nights have always needed celebrating with a well-earned beverage; Lewes even turned the spot of a horrific disaster, the 1836 avalanche in Cliffe (the nation's worst ever), into a commemoration of the event by building a pub on the site. Lewes has a tradition of making the best out of natural and other disasters. The Snowdrop made a place for public gathering, refreshment and entertainment out of the site of a disastrous 1830s' landfall, and Harveys have made beers to commemorate not only the 1980s fire that burned down parts of the brewery (a smoky beer) but also one after it was flooded out, along with most of Lewes, in 2000 (Ouse Booze).

Further back in time, as one of King Alfred's burhs, it would have experienced brewing from at least Saxon times. After the Norman Conquest, Lewes' unique castle (with two mottes) was constructed. The castle would have meant protection and employment, so the town and its number of brewers would have grown. William de Warenne, the town's overlord, who was given the Rape of Lewes in return for his services at Hastings and for building the castle, also built the priory at Lewes. Still a magnificent set of ruins today, the abbots and priors would have brewed beer as their diversion, and their use of the Winterbourne stream shows. The large number of toilets the priors built in their religious complex perhaps suggests they brewed a bit too much of it. The ale they brewed (Bishop's Finger, perhaps, or Abbot's Ale?) would have come in handy when hosting the many visitors, perhaps the most thirsty of which would have been King Henry's forces who billeted there before the Battle of Lewes in 1264. Hopefully, the damage of the town following the battle didn't affect the town's alehouses.

Lewes – Like No Other

Lewes today is a great place for visitors searching for a cosy or welcoming pub like the Snowdrop and its many other nearby boozers. This is the joy of Lewes: there is no huge walk needed to visit a good range of the town's pubs – even if you start at the Snowdrop in Cliffe and make it to the Black Horse, it will be a pleasant and manageable journey, devoid of soulless chain or themed pubs. Instead, the pub-goer gets to enjoy a wide range of hospitable hotels and taverns with conversation audible, not deafening dirges blasting from speakers or wall-to-wall Sky Sports.

Lewes has always been fiercely independent and its unique spectrum of social houses reflects this. It is easily reachable from Brighton and a comfortable jaunt from the capital but the town has resisted acquiring the characteristics of either. Lewes' unusual state as a 'gap town' in the South Downs is equally felt in its pubs – it doesn't feel the need to be like the coastal towns to its south or the cosy Sussex villages to its north, west and east. With no university, Lewes has a more mature crowd of pub-goers, and having a wealthy, friendly, well-educated and fairly political population, you are guaranteed an interesting and welcomed time as a new visitor to Lewes' pubs. You have an historic and fascinating town to explore and, should Lewes' dozen-plus town-centre pubs not be enough, we have included some hotels that feel like pubs and also one coffee bar, The Real Eating Company, which feels like a contemporary, family-friendly pub. For those of you wanting to explore the Weald or Downland around Lewes, we have also taken this book to sample a few picturesque pubs in villages a decent walk from Lewes such as Firle, Glynde and Kingston. As Lewes was once a rest stop on the pilgrims' trail where religious travellers once stopped for ale and food, why not continue this trend and experience a mix of walking, supping and eating?

DID YOU KNOW?

Despite sounding as if we are continuing to discuss eating, Toad in the Hole is, in fact, Lewes' most popular pub game. Lewes has a range of bizarre pub games, with the strangest (Spaniel Racing and Dwyle Flunking) taking place just at the Lewes Arms. However, it is Toad that holds most affection in Lewesians' hearts and appears in most Lewes pubs. Since its resurrection at the end of the twentieth century, there is now even a local league that takes the game seriously. For the uninitiated, you need a table with a tilted slate table top, with a hole in the middle that players need to flip coins into. No sausages, gravy or batter are needed.

Chapter One

Cliffe

1. The Snowdrop Inn, South Street, Cliffe

We start our exploration of Lewes' pubs with a bit of an explanation as to our chosen route here. A start in Cliffe means anyone trying to follow the route of this book will have uphill walking to do, but they embrace, in my view, the best route. Also, with this book commencing with the Snowdrop, this is the first pub the visitor to Lewes encounters as they voyage north up

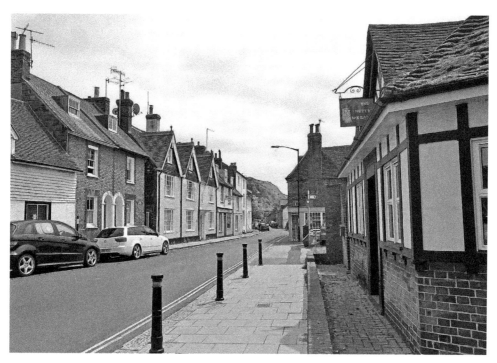

South Street, looking towards the Snowdrop and the site of the 1836 avalanche.

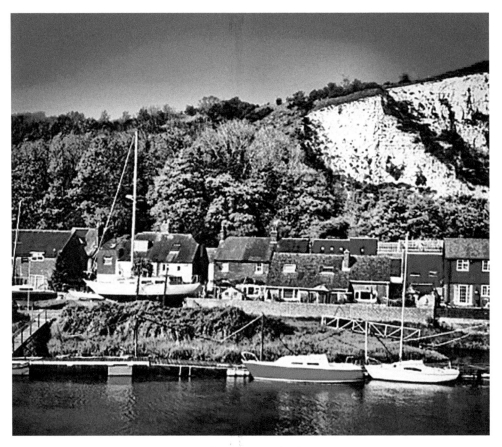

Cliffe looks like a seaside village in this photo, which it was centuries ago.

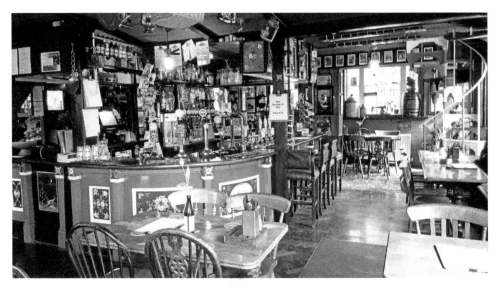

The Snowdrop Inn – bohemian and a cosy place to nurse a beer.
(Courtesy of Gabi Stern)

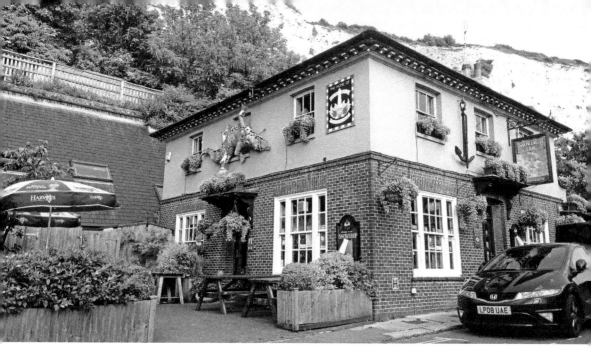

Above: The Snowdrop today, next to the cliffs, the avalanche from which gave the pub its name. (Courtesy of Gabi Stern)

Below: South Street Cliffe, walking away from the Snowdrop towards the Dorset.

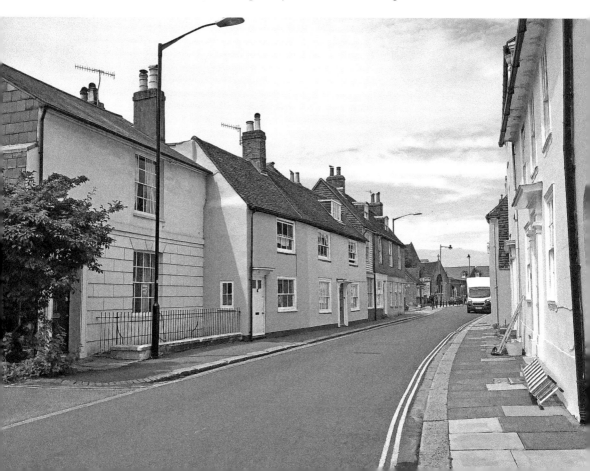

the A26 from the A27 east–west bypass south of the town. This provides those new to Lewes the chance to drive, or preferably walk, along the reason Lewes exists: the Ouse. The Ouse was once far more powerful and wider as its watery forces cut through the chalk downland in this part of Sussex many millennia ago to make Lewes a 'gap town' in the Downs: a rare spot where the Downs simply stop. This meant early travellers along the Downs were forced to come 'a down' (where the hills get their name from). Sussex was wooded and dangerous down below the Downs and the South Downs Way, today still such a loved route for ramblers, was the drovers' 'motorway' of the early Britons. This is why forts existed along its route at Cissbury, the Trundle, Chanctonbury and Caburn. The Ouse cutting through these meant a crossing place was needed, which still exists today across from Cliffe. Where people had to cross, they could be traded with, and so the town developed around the bridge. A huge inland sea flowed inland up the 7 miles from the Ouse's mouth at Seaford (it was rerouted by the 1700s to enter the sea at its current destination at Newhaven – hence the name of New Haven) and so Lewes was in effect, a coastal harbour town, and also the safest and first place you could travel around this large broad-water.

Walking north to the Snowdrop today, the wetlands west of the Ouse still convey the idea of how much wider the river once was (and the views of the castle are inspiring). You start your tour with where Lewes really was once on the coast, the sea encroaching this far inland in a wide estuary. The Ouse is still tidal today. The river bending at Lewes, coupled with a winterbourne stream south of the hill of the town, meant it was a hilltop settlement easier to defend from seaborne invaders, being surrounded by water on two fronts and providing a good view of any invaders taking the route by water (that we now we take on foot or wheels towards the town up the A26). To get to London, invaders could use Sussex's rivers to get inland far quicker than its almost non-existent roads. This is why the Saxons and then the Normans fortified Lewes – you could identify invaders from here and thus prevent them infiltrating inland. Lewes was the first safe settlement at a time when coastal settlements were often destroyed; it was the frontline, but also a trade and transport route. It made obvious sense that a town of importance would develop here.

The move some years back to make South Street in Cliffe a cul-de-sac also made and makes sense too. As the walker leaves the A26 and passes by the barrier to enter from the A26 South Street into non-A26 South Street, they'll notice this once-busy route is now a quiet backstreet with two pubs: the Snowdrop and, north of Cliffe High Street, the Dorset, which is technically in Malling Street. Walking is the best way to get to the Snowdrop as the driver will need to negoitiate the Cuilfail Tunnel before taking a number of left turns to park in Cliffe. Wandering northwards past the cosy cottages and gorgeous Georgian buildings of South Street, it is hard to imagine looking westwards up at peaceful Lewes today when it was once a warlike, fortified burh, glaring at invaders, nor even a bustling county town which it was until the 1880s. It is also hard to imagine that one of Britain's worst (and most unusual) peacetime tragedies occurred at the location of the first of our pubs on our journey, the Snowdrop Inn.

There were once many more inns in Cliffe (nine in 1906) as with its westwards neighbour, Lewes. Cliffe has lost the King & Queen (named after William and Mary and later called the White Swan), the Swan from at least 1633, the Bear, the Wheatsheaf, the Coombe and the Cricketers, which had an interestingly lofty hillside perch. Riverside pubs long gone include the Bargeman and the Schooner. Other lost pubs included the Thatched House, the Old Ship, the Tanner's Arms in Malling Street and the Anchor. The Snowdrop hasn't always been the site of a pub however, and compared with its more northerly neighbour, the Dorset, the oldest surviving pub in Lewes, it is a mere baby, being built in 1840. Today a bed and breakfast as well as a cosy pub with two side gardens, it was built to commemorate the eight people killed and many injured when a huge overhang of snow on the adjacent sloping cliffs that Cliffe takes its name from fell onto South Street cottages on 27 December 1836. This was Britain's worst ever avalanche and could have been avoided if the cottage dwellers below had heeded the warnings of the danger of being engulfed by the huge expanse of snow above. The white dress worn by one of the survivors, two-year-old Fanny Boakes, during her rescue, is still on view today at Lewes' Anne of Cleves museum.

I would be equally reluctant to leave the Snowdrop today even if a huge overhang of snow threatened to crush the pub, just as it did the preceding cottages on the site. This is such a friendly and cosy boozer with great beers and decent pub grub. The only possible danger to life these days at the Snowdrop is the treacherous staircase, which one reviewer on www.yelp.co.uk described as a dangerous journey, 'especially after a few vinos'. Owned by the same company as the very popular Hop Poles pub in Brighton, it is in the *Telegraph*'s guide for the best British pubs and received an excellent review from them in 2014. It sells the excellent Burning Sky Brewery ales (which has only travelled from the nearby picturesque village of Firle).

The Snowdrop has the wonderful central island bar in the pub, where the excesses of wooden panelling and wood do indeed, as the *Telegraph* says, make it feel like a 'massive log cabin' and certainly a bohemian one at that. The Snowdrop attracts an eclectic mix of locals, students, walkers and arty-types. It was the bohemian nature of the Snowdrop that attracted owners D'Arcy Ganda and his wife Tanya, who bought the pub back in 2004. They told the author of the 2004 book, *Our Lewes*, that buying the Snowdrop 'was just a temptation too good to resist'.

Our Lewes also discusses the previous owners, Tim and Sue May, who gave the pub its bohemian character. As David Sykes recalls in the book: 'There were all sorts of wonderful, mad, gorgeous things to be seen there. A lot of the most interesting young out-of-work people in Lewes found the Snowdrop their natural home – a lot of them were the sort who'd opted out of the rat race.' Sykes is right, the only thing racing about the Snowdrop is the A26, less than 100 metres from this cosy pub, which is still today a lively and cosy pub and a vital part of the Lewes pub scene. It also has possibly one of the country's worst puns as its title in regards to our worst-ever snow- and gravity-related disaster.

2. The Dorset, Malling Street

At first it seems bizarre to have a pub nestled deep within the very heart of Sussex named after a county from the West Country but it makes sense when you know that the Sackville family, who were earls of Dorset had major links with the town. Once renamed as the Manxman, it was reopened by Harveys Brewery last decade with its original name. It is locally known as the 'Cats' by many, due to the leopards on the pub's sign, from the Sackville family's coat of arms. The Dorset is very much a Sussex pub however, being a Harveys Brewery pub with the venerable ale on tap and also in being home of the Cliffe Bonfire Society. The society uses the Dorset on many occasions for fundraising, such as Harvest Festival and a lively New Year's Eve party, not to forget the events of the 4–6 November when Lewes becomes the world's most dedicated spot to commemorate the arrest and execution of the Catholics who plotted to

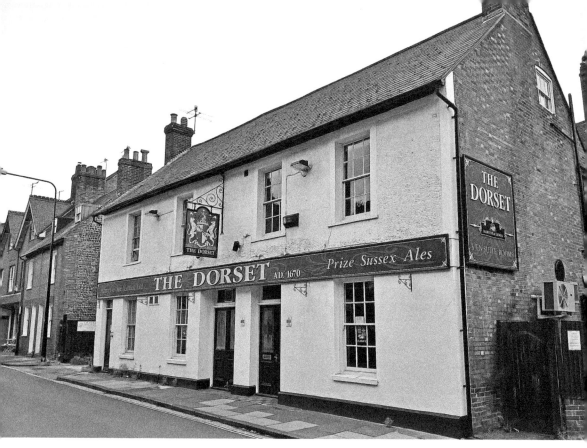

Above: The Dorset, the only remaining pub in this part of Cliffe.

Below: The Dorset's beer garden. *Inset*: The Dorset's dining room.

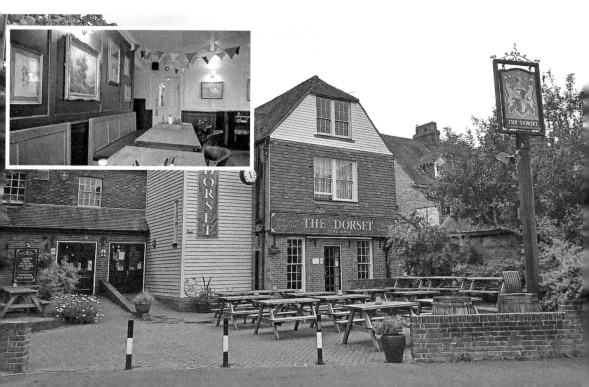

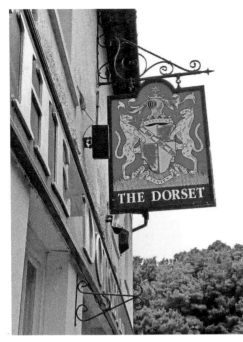

Left: The Dorset's pub sign.

Below: Chapel Hill. The starting point for a great walk from the Dorset.

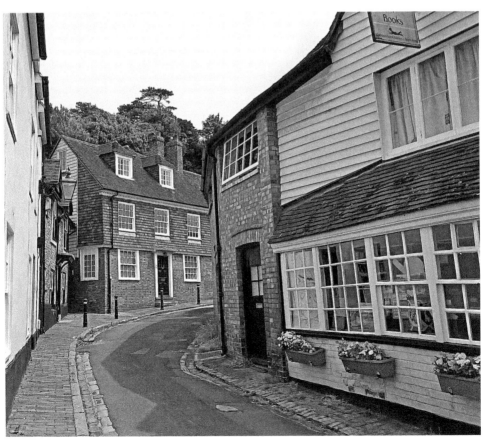

destroy Parliament in 1605. Mementoes of past Bonfire nights include life-sized effigies of the Pope and Guy Fawkes, who have somehow survived past burnings and customers can now sit and have a pint next to them. Alongside Parliament, another ancient English tradition that is in evidence at the Dorset is Morris dancing, and the pub hosts the celebration of the Morris Men at several points throughout the year. Back in the 1700s, entertainment for customers also involved outdoor activities, in the guise of Mr and Mrs Phillip Astley's performing horses.

Paul and Rob Palmer (the latter was also the chef during my visit) provide a family-friendly pub that is in the heart of the eastern side of Cliffe, looking up at the Cliff itself. Good beer, the Six Nations on the telly and Rob's Dorset signature snack, the Dorset Toastie, all added up to a hugely pleasant experience which was enjoyed partly in the pub's tastefully decorated dining room. The toastie is a wonderful concoction that is heartily recommended, a New York homage full of pastrami, gherkins, and Monterey Jack cheese, complemented with chips and salad. Perhaps a New York visit inspired the snack?

Another type of visit has been experienced at the Dorset, of the spiritual kind, as you might expect in Cliffe's oldest pub, built in 1670. The pub has six guest rooms upstairs and when these rooms have been empty, the housekeepers have reported voices and seen the odd peculiar shadow. Thankfully nothing too creepy, the voices just seem to be women chatting. Perhaps they're wondering how effigies of the Pope and Guy Fawkes survived a Lewes Bonfire Night.

The Dorset has something for everyone: history, Harveys beer, pleasant dining areas, a roaring fire in the winter and an ample beer garden patio for warmer months with hog roasts and barbeques. Dogs and families are welcome and with the wonderful walk up Chapel Hill to the Downs that all visitors must take a minute away, it's tricky to find anything to dislike about the Dorset. With six guest rooms upstairs it means visitors don't have too far to wander at the end of their evening, either.

3. The Real Eating Company, Cliffe High Street

Including the Real Eating Company may seem like a bit of a cheat in a guide to Lewes' pubs but this is an independent restaurant and coffee shop with many features that make it seem like a bright and airy contemporary drinking den. It believes in great food and most importantly serves excellent local craft beers and decent wine as well

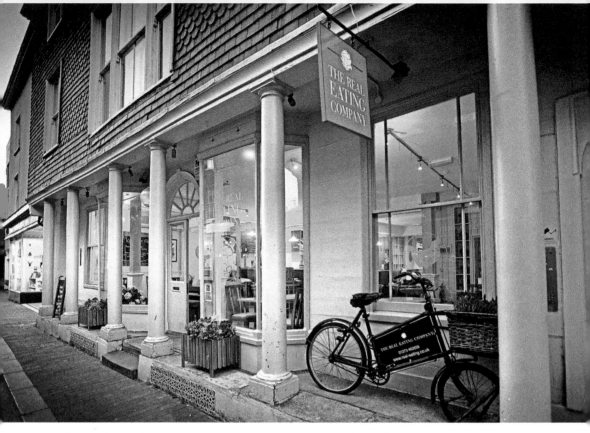

Above: The Real Eating Company: not a pub, but a good spot for tasty food and craft beer.

Below: Cliffe High Street, home of the Gardener's and the Real Eating Company.

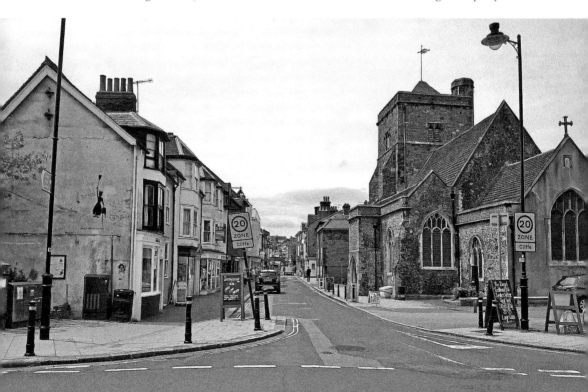

as a range of fresh, ready-to-go food, on site every day. The Real Eating Company was created by Helena Hudson in January 2004. Helena moved to Brighton from London in 2001 with her family and quickly spotted the potential for a high-quality British casual-dining café concept in the South East. Situated on Cliffe High Street, it is a good choice for the family who wants to avoid the more traditional Lewes pubs and characters that can frequent them, even at lunchtimes. During my visit, there were several weary fathers with youngsters fast asleep in their buggies, giving dad a chance to sneak a cheeky pint and read the paper in peace. New and sleep-deprived fathers in Cliffe need their place for a family-friendly pint, and the REC is that place.

4. The Gardener's Arms, Cliffe High Street

The Gardener's Arms is pretty unique as a little pub that relies on its regulars supping gallons of (usually real) ale as it is that rarity of a 'wet' pub lacking a food menu. Thankfully this narrow drinking den has plenty of thirsty beer-drinking regulars who know and like their beer, ensuring the pub continues to survive. The Gardener's, also found in

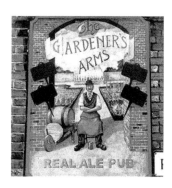

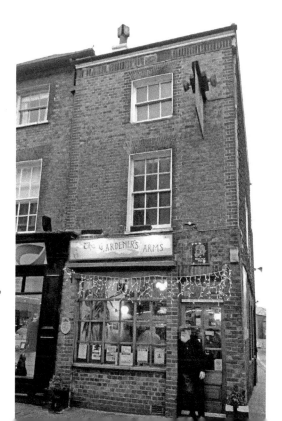

Right: The Gardener's Arms exterior, 2016, complete with typical 'gardener'.

Above: The Gardener's sign.

the very pretty high street of Cliffe, is something therefore of a survivor, not only by relying on ale sales alone, but having survived the early twentieth-century cull of pubs that left it as the only pub in this part of Cliffe after the Bear burnt down in 1918. The best phrase I've heard to describe the Gardener's is that what it lacks in space it makes up for in character; this is certainly true. When visiting there with workmates a few years ago, knowing one of the regulars (who was also a workmate) meant that this little local suddenly became full of plenty of characters whom we seemed to know too. The friendly welcome isn't just from the regulars either. The staff are very knowledgeable and help you choose your beer, which can be a task as the Gardener's is certainly a real ale lover's pub. Reviewers of the pub love its small nature and friendly character but also see it as a hindrance. One visitor said: '[It is] tight for space, you have to climb over people to get to the toilet, toilet strategy helps, especially if there is a darts match.' This is the only time I have ever heard the phrase 'toilet strategy' used. It is also the only pub about which I have read the following comment: 'The side door helps if your [sic] claustrophobic.' The Gardener's has one other unique feature for Lewes – it is the only pub that doesn't actively welcome children. So for a guaranteed child-free zone, the Gardener's Arms is the complete opposite to its opposite neighbour, the Real Eating Company.

5. The John Harvey Tavern, Bear Lane, off Cliffe High Street

The John Harvey Tavern has confused many who think it is a much more established drinking den than it actually is due to its home in the old stables of the long-gone Bear Inn and outbuildings of Harveys Brewery. As its location suggests, it was indeed in the vicinity of the much older Bear Inn, which was Lewes' premier waterside pub (as well as acting as its town hall at times) from the 1500s until its destruction by fire in 1918. This was nothing to do with the war, but one of a number of unfortunate fires (some of which were arson) that Lewes has faced. Perhaps the worst of these was the Harveys Brewery fire in the 1980s, the result of a nasty arson attack. The Bear was Cliffe's largest inn and an important meeting place, and it boasted that on market days its stables could accommodate forty horses.

The pub could not be better named though, as the brewery 'tap' for its brewery across the road, but also as the location in the south of Bear

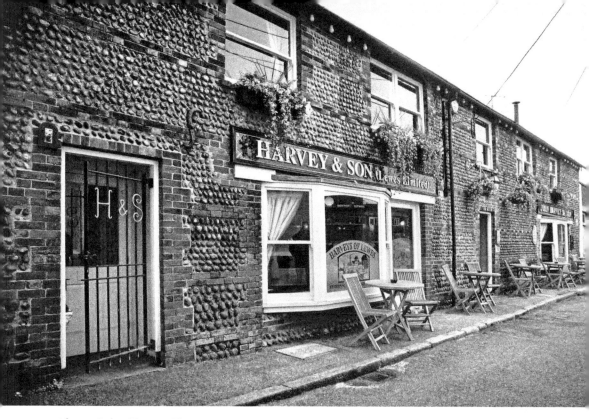

Above: John Harvey Tavern, 2016.

Below: John Harvey Tavern, the Lewes Room.
Inset: The function room.

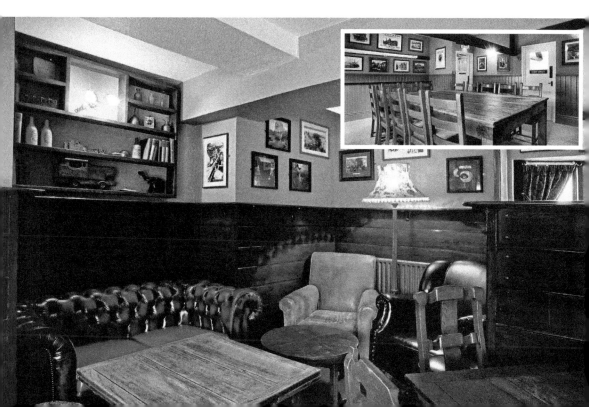

Lane where John Harvey had his original brewery, south of Cliffe High Street at the Cliffe Tavern opposite the Bear. This was when he changed from selling wines in the 1790s to brewing beer. Harveys went from strength to strength after the brewery crossed the road and moved to its current riverside location. During the 1980s, the stables were renovated and opened as a restaurant with the poor attempt at a humorous name of the Weighed Inn. The horrific fire at the Harveys brewery in 1996 meant that the one-time stables were needed by office staff at the brewery on a temporary basis. Once the brewery was restored to its former glory in 1998, the Bear Lane site reopened, but this time as the John Harvey Tavern, or 'JHT' as it can be known.

Today, it has a very welcoming atmosphere and, as you would expect, serves up a fine selection of Harveys ales. Its website proudly boasts that the staff are credited with being 'the most helpful (but, most of all, the cutest!) in Lewes'. Just who judged this isn't clear. For a small, narrow pub, it does manage to cram a lot in, with regular live music nights including Jazz Night on a Wednesday. The bar boasts wooden beams, a log burner and wine vats, where you can tuck yourself away for a cosy chat. There is also the History Room, with pictures of Cliffe High Street dating back to the early nineteenth century. Unlike the nearby Gardeners, children are allowed in restaurant areas but not actually in the bar. Children do better than dogs though, which aren't allowed upstairs in the restaurant at all. With the Bear Inn now not even a memory to Lewes' oldest residents, having burnt down nearly a century ago, the JHT is the nearest Lewes has to a riverside pub, a real surprise in a town where the Ouse dominates the landscape so much and with riverside pubs much in vogue. Imagine an equivalent of Arundel's Black Rabbit in the town, or even in the old Railway Land? Chorlton in south Manchester has an amazing riverside pub that is worth a similar walk.

Chapter Two

Lewes – North of the High Street

6. The Volunteer, Eastgate Street

Crossing over Cliffe Bridge we now enter Lewes, which most people don't really consider much of a boundary these days but there was once much rivalry between the two towns, even having rival fire brigades at one point. This may stem back from the fact that Lewes and Cliffe were in two separate territories (or 'rapes' as the Normans called them, named after the way the county was 'roped' off) – Cliffe was administered from distant Pevensey. Not until 1881 were Cliffe and South Malling incorporated into the borough of Lewes, ending the autonomy residents had enjoyed over their own affairs since the Saxon era.

The Volunteer, or 'Volly' as it was known by older generations, is sited in one of Lewes' busiest locations, being on the inner ring road with traffic constantly rushing past. Despite this, it makes the most of its beer garden and the building it is based in is a gorgeous example of Lewes architecture, dating from the early 1800s, which probably explains its name, relating to the volunteer soldiers needed to fight Napoleon at that time. It would be best described as a plain-and-simple town pub that doesn't quite seem to suit Lewes, possibly as it seems to have a lively and student-y crowd, making you feel more like you're in Western Road in Brighton. You couldn't exactly call it a gastropub, but the fare is simple and tasty and drinks are fairly cheap for the South East.

7. The Crown Hotel, Market Street/School Hill

From the Volly to the Crown involves Lewes' steepest climb, which gives the walker a good thirst for the first pub at the top as there is no

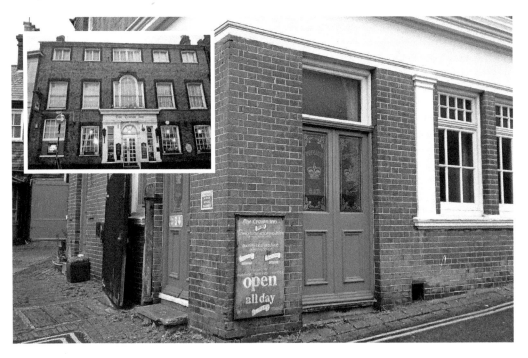

Above: The Crown Shades: the front was for the wealthy and well-to-do, the rear for the poorer locals.
Inset: The Crown exterior. Lewes' faded jewel in the crown, with so much potential.

Below: The Crown's Winter Garden and Shades.
Inset: The Victorian must-have for all-year sunshine.

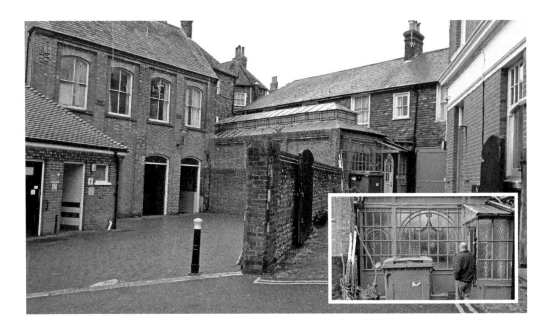

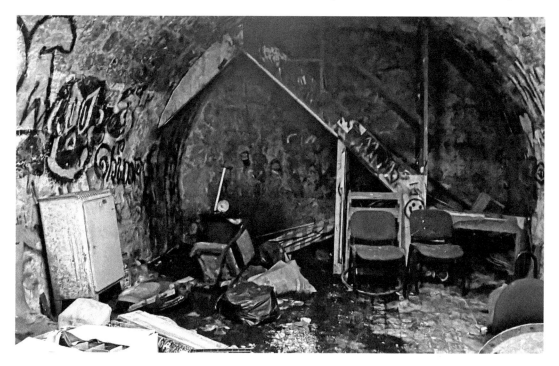

The Crown's western cellar, a '90s party place and underground haunted hotspot.

stop anywhere for a pint while ascending School Hill. Lewes needs a good pub on the way up the steep yet wonderfully imposing School Hill, whose name is apparently nothing to do with schools, but from the old English for shoe. The Crown has seen better days but is an important part of the very heart of town, as the Crown Hotel has been offering a warm welcome to its customers for over 350 years. Built in the reign of Charles I, the Crown Inn occupies a commanding position but feels like it is running only on two valves. It could be Lewes' boutique hotel and has the space to rival the White Hart for expansion, with a Victorian conservatory, numerous back rooms and its hotel rooms fully booked out with long-term residents. Sadly its current owners, Enterprise Inns, don't seem to want to spend any money transforming a hotel with so much to offer. Yet they should – visiting the Crown feels like an adventure when you are within its panelled walls. It has locals that make you welcome while feeling you are in a mix of Ealing and Simon Pegg/ Nick Frost films. Its 'Winter Garden' from the mid-Victorian era would make a wonderful place to dine and the neglected Victorian dining room to the west of it would also be a much-loved drinking or dining room.

The earliest mention of the inn was as the home of the wealthy Spicer family but had become the Black Lyon in 1638 when Henry Townsend was the landlord. By 1790 the wonderfully named Joseph Spittle changed the name to the Crown Inn and rebuilt the front facade. It lived up to its new name in the 1830 when William VI, while in residence at the Royal Pavilion, entertained at the Crown, at a time when it was apparently serving as a high-class brothel. The pub has several claims to fame, firstly as Lewes' oldest continually serving licensed house, since at least the 1630s and possibly back to 1610. It is claimed to be the most haunted pub in Sussex, with reported poltergeist activity and the presence of an evil religious figure who sits on the steps of the cellar. The cellar, to the south-west of the conservatory, feels older than the pub and has apparently been used by modern witches as well as for 1980s and '90s parties judging by the rough decorating inside. No tunnels can be found today that once may have been connected to the castle, but it is likely that the pub sits above medieval vaults. Whether all of this background gives reason to its apparent supernatural happenings is anyone's guess, but the barman back in 2010 refused to go down to the cellar on his own, according to everythingghost.co.uk who undertook an impromptu investigation of the pub when staying there to investigate Brighton's Preston Manor. The barman also stated how the hotel bell would move up and down and ring of its own accord, and apparitions have been seen by staff and residents. A woman in grey that the staff call 'Emily' also moves about the hotel, as well as one of a man in a brown jacket by the old bureau in Room 5. Whatever the spirits are protesting about, I'd gladly bet it's that they're fuming that such a historically rich, architecturally splendid and potentially amazing high street hotel is so under-utilised. The Crown has so much potential, character, personality and could be the jewel in Lewes' crown.

8. The Star, High Street

Worthing once had its town hall in a pub. So did Lewes, but now one of its pubs is the town hall. The Star was once one of Lewes' major inns and is famed today as the site outside of which ten of the seventeen Sussex Protestant martyrs were burned to death. One of the seventeen, Deryk Carver from Brighton was a Flemish brewer who had immigrated to Britain and had set up the Black Lion Brewery in Brighton, the black lion being part of the emblem of his home country of Flanders (Belgium today).

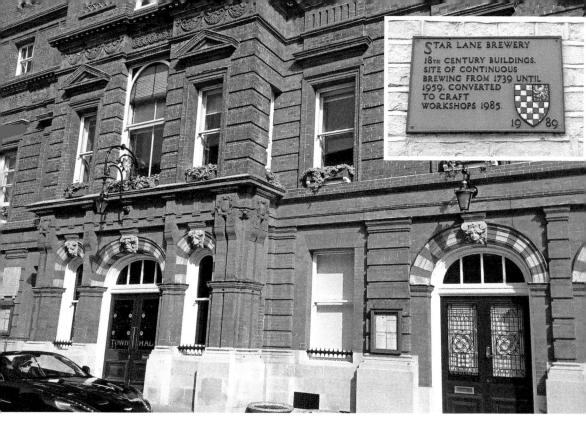

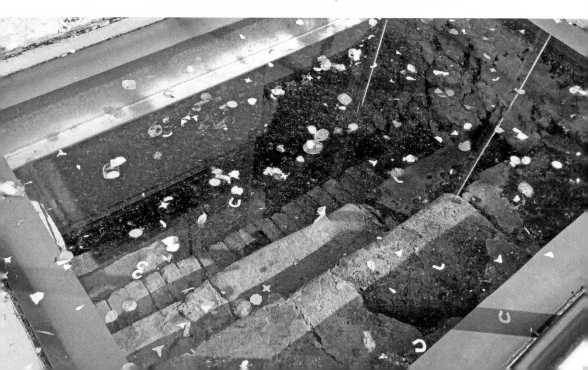

Above: Lewes Town Hall, reminding us that it was once a pub with a Star sign and the faces of Bacchus above the door. *Inset*: Sign commemorating the Star Lane Brewery's former location; the Lamb is just visible in the foreground.

Below: The enclosed medieval steps down to what was the Star's cellars that the martyrs would have climbed before their deaths by fire outside the Star.

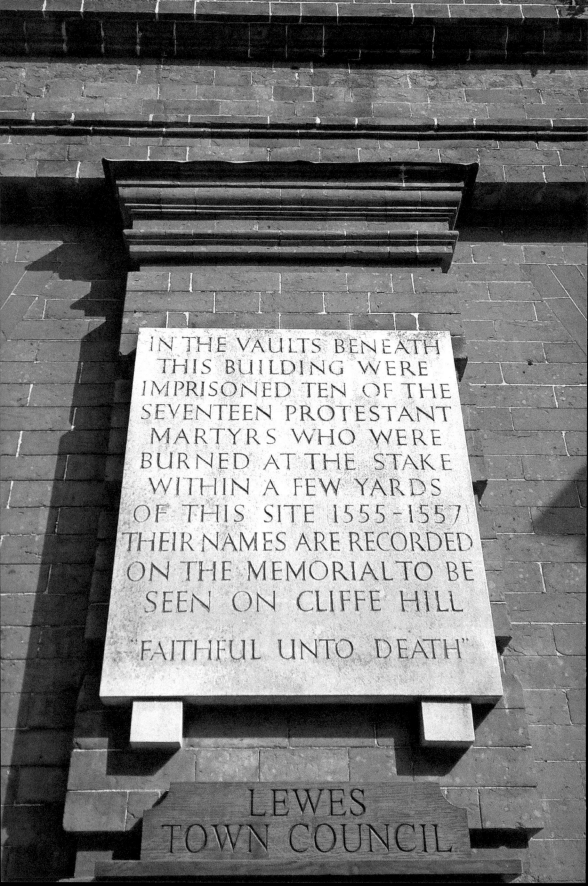

IN THE VAULTS BENEATH
THIS BUILDING WERE
IMPRISONED TEN OF THE
SEVENTEEN PROTESTANT
MARTYRS WHO WERE
BURNED AT THE STAKE
WITHIN A FEW YARDS
OF THIS SITE 1555-1557
THEIR NAMES ARE RECORDED
ON THE MEMORIAL TO BE
SEEN ON CLIFFE HILL

"FAITHFUL UNTO DEATH"

LEWES
TOWN COUNCIL

Carver was burned in a barrel, unlike the others, to mock his 'lowly' occupation, although at that time a brewer was a wealthy and skilled trade. The Star is today Lewes' Town Hall (as opposed to the County Hall, further west) and a sign commemorates the death of the martyrs, whose death was ordered by Tudor queen 'Bloody' Mary. The memorial facing the Town Hall is Lewes' war memorial but to find the memorial to the martyrs you need to look east across the Ouse Valley to the hills above Cliffe where the Victorian-era memorial is situated, also in the shape of an obelisk.

The Protestants were kept in the vaults below the Star Inn before their flaming execution and so spent their last hours underneath the town's prominent tavern of the 1500s. Lewes Council has recently revealed the steps to the cellars the martyrs would have climbed, now covered with a glass viewing panel. This one-time pub cellar would make the most atmospheric of clubs or bars today, despite or perhaps because of its gruesome past. Why not a bar called the Martyrs?

Pub cellars had a range of uses in the days before our modern era, one of which was equally gruesome. People don't realise that the places where their wooden casks of Harveys or Dark Star are now kept cool were, in the days before refrigeration, mortuaries, especially before inquests. Corpses were regularly kept below floors of pubs to delay decomposition.

Talking of stars, the Star Inn's choice of symbol was due to Lewes being part of a pilgrim's trail from Canterbury to Winchester, and the High Street through the town and into Cliffe being an ancient route for religious travellers. Star inns, like Lewes', and Alfriston's were places for these travellers to rest with the 'star' symbol lighting their way, like the star in the nativity. This makes it unsurprising that the original building dated back over 650 years and was originally the home of the well-to-do Spicer family. Like other Lewes pubs, it was also the home of two MPs for Lewes, both part of the Spicer family. The location of the Star Inn also reminds us that the star was also linked, later on, to the nearby Star Brewery, which is now part of the 'Needlemakers' complex of quirky shops, tea rooms and galleries. The building that housed the Star Brewery is now a gallery and creative studio. The Star would have acted as the Brewery Tap. The Town Hall that replaced the Star Inn was built in 1893 and has a motif in its architecture that reminds us of its previous use as a pub from at least the 1500s: the figure of Bacchus, god of wine appears on a keystone on the building. When asked, the majority of Lewes' ratepayers were against the conversion of the Star but appear to have been ignored by the council, who made the decision to demolish the historic pub. Thankfully, once a year the Star returns from pub heaven – sort of – as the Town Hall hosts the annual Lewes Beer Festival in June. Beer, cider and other drinks are once more poured at the site of one of Lewes' oldest hostelries. If we count this, Lewes' hotels and the Real Eating Company, Lewes actually has more than twenty drinking places and has only lost the Meridian in the last decade.

DID YOU KNOW?

Lewes has lost eight breweries to history and numerous pubs. Every taxi driver seems to have a different number of how many there used to be, forty-two being a number that was bandied about on my last visit, which theoretically must have been correct at some point as sixty-three pubs have closed since the town's peak in 1887. Some of Lewes' lost pubs include (most recently in 2010 the Meridian, formerly the Pewter Pot), and also in no particular order, the Dolphin Inn, the Fruiterers, the Beerhouse at Chalk Pit Cottages, the Unicorn, the Bear, the Wheatsheaf, the Coombe, the Beehive, the Hare & Hounds and the Cricketers. The King & Queen must have been incredible, built in 1694 almost opposite the Dorset when the Bear in Cliffe featured performances of John Gay's *The Beggar's Opera*, performed by one man who impersonated all the characters and provided all the voices. Despite its name, the Bear, which was next to the river until it burnt down in 1918, had no bear-baiting that was instead hosted at the Coombe. For those who liked their blood sport more of the feathery kind, the Wheatsheaf was Lewes' centre for cock-fighting.

The Bear would be a more feasible and ethically focused pub to contemplate rebuilding, as it was on Lewes' most potentially exciting site with its riverside and central location at the very heart of Lewes and Cliffe: Cliffe Bridge. Hopefully, Lewesophiles everywhere will come together to demand the demolition of the horrible Argos building and its replacement with a replica of the old coaching inn, which was such an important part of the Cliffe. Shockingly, Lewes has no truly riverside pub, the nearest being the distant glimpse JHT customers get, a closer view needing them to drag their chairs across Bear Yard. A 'New Bear' would be hugely desirable and would celebrate Lewes' defining feature: the Ouse.

One of the most interesting lost pubs of Lewes must be the Crimean Tavern, which existed at No. 15 Lancaster Street, on the site of the Little Theatre. It was demolished in the 1950s but it enjoyed a long and interesting existence, being opened a decade after the war it was named after, with the first landlord being Thomas Huggett who ran it until 1880. The name derived not just in commemoration of the war but, it is believed, by the nearby naval prison in North Street where approximately 400 Finnish prisoners were kept during the Crimean War after the fall of the Russian fortress of Bomarsund. The licensing authorities in Lewes refused to let Annie Verrall, the widow of the last-ever landlord run the pub, despite her illustrious surname being linked with that much-loved of brewers. This must have been a cruel turn of events less than a year after the mysterious death of her husband, John Alfred Verrall, in 1921. It was probably part of the review of the

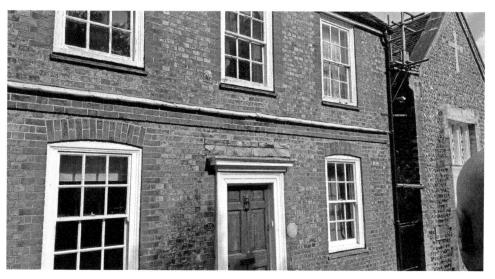

The Britannia Inn, Keere Street, a private dwelling today in Lewes' famous street.

number of licences of smaller premises in the town in the early twentieth century, and by that time she too must have been of advanced years herself. In February 1921, at the age of sixty-four, Alfred Verrall drowned in the Ouse at a point called Captain's Hole, opposite Malling's church. He had been on a ramble, walking his dog and had been ill for some time, as well as only having one eye. The mysterious death may have been linked to his illness, but no clue was ever discovered and the verdict on his death was 'found drowned'.

9. The Lamb, Fisher Street

Within a pea's throw from the Lewes Arms, it's only right that a town with centuries of sheep-farming heritage, nestled deep in the sheep-covered South Downs, celebrates our four-legged woolly friends. Not that the Lamb is a farmer's pub, but instead an usual mix of unusual bar running along the entire length of the pub on the left and large cavernous function room that hosts Lewes' more musical events. Lewes obviously needs live music venues but it does mean that the place feels a bit odd at other times and isn't necessarily the first choice for the drinker after a cosy, quiet pint, but if you do yearn for this then there is a small, snug area by the large fireplace. The Lamb does tend to be quiet too when there's no music on. There is also a large outdoor area which is great for the summer and its ales seem to be popular, which is one of its charms, along with its rustic, barn-like feel and exposed brickwork. It's this mix of features that make the Lamb a bit hard to define; its most definable feature is probably that of a music venue and it could almost be seen as two pubs in one. As the headquarters of the Waterloo Bonfire Society, perhaps the Lamb needs to celebrate this more?

10. The Elephant & Castle, White Hill

The Pells is said to feel like a village within the town of Lewes, with the Church of St John sub Castro nearby which makes the 'Elly' a village pub to the people of the Pells. Landlord and landlady Huw and Hannah Jones are very proud of this and that the Elly is first and foremost still a genuine pub, which is family run and open to everyone. It is indeed a welcoming place to everyone, and a much-used meeting place and social centre for Lewes folk. Mums and dads of newborns and young children have National Childbirth groups on offer in the pub. The pub works hard to support local charities and organisations, giving up space to the Commercial Square Bonfire Society as well as other good causes. This society has used the pub as their meeting place ever since their inception. This is indeed a proud claim in a town that values its Bonfire Society so highly.

The Elephant & Castle has had much history since its foundation stone was laid back on 22 September 1838. It has hosted numerous breweries before the current suppliers, Enterprise Inns, including Unique, Pheonix, Tamplins, East Grinstead and originally South Downs who built the building. There is much uncertainty about the origins of the pub's name. The area in London called the Elephant and Castle is said to be an Anglicisation of the title 'Infanta de Castile', dating back to medieval marriages of royalty, but this makes little sense to a central Sussex town. There has been some argument that it was a reference to the earliest brewery's logo, but Huw, the current landlord, makes much sense with his argument that as it's situated on the route to the capital, it may well have links to its London namesake.

One thing Lewes shares with London is that public hangings were once commonplace, and Lewes' took place just near the current site of the Elly at Abinger Place. Many years back there was a story that the pub had an underground passage to the site of the gallows, coming out into Hangman's Acre, adjoining Paddock Road. Still today there is a stone in the wall to remind wrongdoers of where people were hanged. In the days prior to refrigeration, it was vital that bodies were kept cool before to burial and so they were apparently carried away to the Elly's cellars. Having the tunnel also meant that when there was a spot of bother at the execution, the bodies could be quickly smuggled away. Huw says one part of the Elly's cellars still have a blocked-up area, which lends ammunition to the argument behind such a tunnel.

Moving up to the ground floor of the pub today, like the King's Head, it has a central island bar in the middle of the pub which always seems the cosiest and friendliest layout for pubs. A small bar and two function rooms behind can be hired out for meetings, private parties and buffets. The Elly claims it has the grandest pub function room in Lewes, which is based upon its high ceiling, open fireplace and chandeliers. This could lead to a pub-to-pub clash of the function rooms, should the Royal Oak

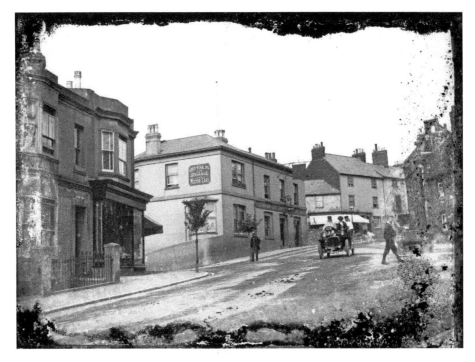

Above: The Elephant & Castle, 1920s. (Courtesy of Huw Jones, landlord)

Below: The Elly at the start of the Blair years; things could only get better.
Inset: The Bottle and Jug section of the Elly in the 1940s; obviously a thirsty time.

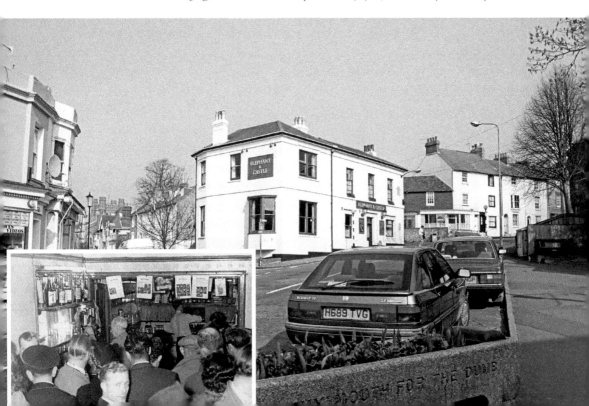

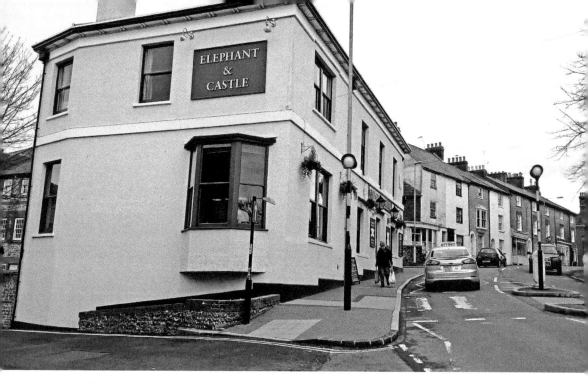

The Elly today, one of Lewes' great community pubs, and which once chucked out Norman Baker.

decide to counter that claim with its equally palatial assembly room, although admittedly theirs is almost a secret.

The Elly has numerous TV screens so customers have no chance of missing sporting action; it is one of the few pubs to show sport in Lewes, sometimes more than one game at once, and it claims a fantastic atmosphere on match days. On my last visit this was certainly the case, and thankfully the pub was without the loutish crowds that some 'sports pubs' can attract. The love of sport is reflected in the pub's website which seems to be the go-to location for Lewes sports news and updates, and of course there is the ubiquitous Toad game available. Despite being so large, the pub does get very busy, especially for major sports events. The clientele consists mainly of genial, generally twenty- to forty-somethings on these days, and customers of all ages at other times.

Food seems to be a pub strength, with many of the friendly football crowd in at the time I last visited heartily tucking into the pub's well-known range of eleven burgers. Some of these have the best names you will find: a 'Smelly Elly', the patty topped with stilton; the 'Anti-social Elly' topped with garlic mayo; and my favourite, the 'Piggy Elly', garnished with a rasher of bacon. Beer is not neglected at the cost of food however, with the Elly having a craft beer menu with over sixty beers from all around the world (including my favourite, Yeastie Boys, from New Zealand) as well being unique in Lewes for having its own microbrewery on the premises. It is worth trying the lovely spicy ginger beer they brew, as well as a 'lovely hopped IPA'. The beer menu is constantly updated and includes the latest ten new brews most recently in.

The beer may be aimed at the latest demands in the drinks market and brewed using state-of-the-art techniques, but at least one of the figures to spend time in the pub may be supernaturally old. Huw reports that numerous customers have 'seen and heard things' and recounts how 'one night I was having a drink after hours and heard someone coming down the stairs; I went to check and found nothing. The person I was with also heard the noise. This happened two more times before we both decided it was time to leave the "ghost" to its own devices.' The ghost seems never to have performed this trick while the pub is busy, which it often is.

The pub's busy state is because customers genuinely enjoy themselves. There must certainly have been a very enjoyable celebration after the pub's rugby team played London Irish back in 1992. Today it is still an enjoyable and lively place, with a vibrant atmosphere for all ages, helped by having regulars who are local celebrities, famous opera singers, conductors and musicians. However, one group of musicians who weren't appreciated by the previous landlord was Norman Baker's band. The former local Lewes MP, who also moonlighted as an amateur musician, must have wronged the governor musically as he was turfed out halfway through the set, with the guv saying he didn't like their music. It is hard to imagine this happening today under current genial landlords who have made the pub a friendly and welcoming community pub, management who are willing to do everything it takes to make the Elly a home from home and who work tirelessly to make their house a special public house.

11. The Lewes Arms, Castle Precincts

For a town that can be rowdy, radical and rambunctious, it is only right that the pub bearing the name Lewes Arms matches this. It is a wonderful pub, which will remind visiting or exiled Brightonians of the Cricketers in Brighton's Lanes, that seems to court controversy and conflict, which makes it all the more interesting. Still today, this Fuller's pub states

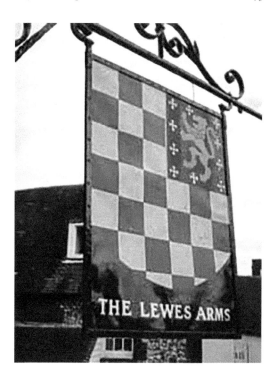

Lewes Arms, 2016, the only pub in Britain next to a dual-motte Norman castle. *Inset*: Lewes Arms sign today: even this caused controversy and conflict.

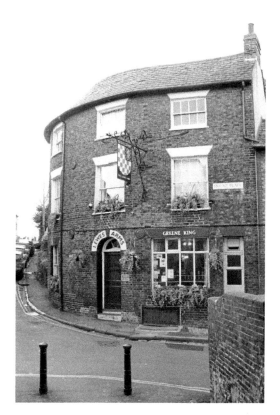

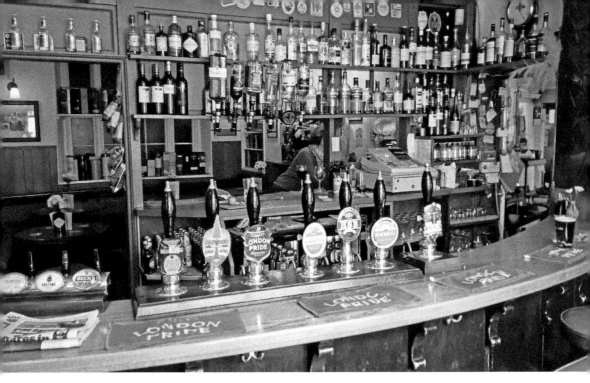

Lewes Arms front bar today: Harveys still on sale, revolution in Lewes still on hold.

on its website that 'the Lewes Arms reigns supreme as the best pub in Lewes'. No modesty at all there, nor the claim that it is a 'legendary establishment more than two hundred and twenty years in the making'. There is some truth however in the claim that it is the 'famous ale house of the historic town of Lewes' due to the Greene King controversy last decade which meant it was featured in international publications and even on CNN.

Back in 2006, national brewers Greene King, the Lewes Arms' brewery chain at the time and who are based in Bury St Edmunds in Suffolk, made several threats that they would stop serving Lewes' very own Harveys as their own beers, they claimed, were equally good. This was despite Harveys outselling GK's own brands several times over. When the ban was actually implemented, a furore broke out that was badly handled by Greene King, which resulted in a picket line, complaints from the local MP at the time, Norman Baker (the reject musician) and one of the greatest works of genius of all time in the world of protest – a disloyalty card. Disgruntled and self-exiled Lewes Arms' regulars were given a card for rival publicans to stamp so they could tot up how much would have been spent in the Lewes Arms each time they bought a rival pint of Harveys, and was being spent in non-GK pubs. The pub, which was once a Harveys pub anyway back in the 1970s, became a no-go zone, its empty bars hitting not just Greene King's profits (which dived 90 per cent), but its reputation in the town. Still today, the Tally Ho in Landport and the Royal Oak are the only Greene King pubs left and both were near empty on my last visit. Greene King seems not to have learnt from their mistakes at the Lewes Arms and still don't sell Harveys in these pubs, which might account for their emptiness when I visited.

The move to stop stocking Harveys resulted in a light-hearted threat by the Lewes-based brewer to buy up pubs in Bury St Edmunds and immediately rid them of all Greene King brands in direct retaliation. The threat was probably only light-hearted though as Harveys' head brewer Miles Jenner was trained at Greene King. The level of anger reached monumental proportions and Greene King, who ignored pressure from the press and locals for several months, found an effigy of themselves (as an evil 'Green King') being burnt at the Bonfire celebrations that year. One Harveys drinker even vehemently told the *Argus*: 'I will never touch a pint of Greene King and to be honest they can go screw themselves.' They still seemed not to listen even when more than 1,200 people signed petitions and voiced protest at the move. Eventually Lewes MP Norman Baker intervened to broker a deal. Even the usually affable Lewes MP ended up criticising the brewery for being 'inflexible', adding that it all left 'a very bitter taste in the mouth, but sadly not that of Harveys'.

Greene King eventually backtracked and its chairman admitted: 'We underestimated the depth of feeling and level of reaction about our initial decision and I believe that the conclusion the team put forward to return Harveys to the bar is the right one.' Greene King's hopes that the regulars would come back and its reputation in the town fully repaired never seemed to be achieved as only months later Greene King quietly sold the pub to Fuller's, so ever since then it has been owned by the same brewers who own the excellent Basketmakers Arms in Brighton, another pub similar to the Lewes Arms. It is of some wonder why Harveys didn't try and buy back the pub that had once been one of their tied houses, especially after all the national publicity about the loyalty of its customers drinking habits. You can see why loyalty is a feature that regulars were so willing to demonstrate in the Lewes Arms. Heaven help anyone who ever tried to close down the pub. It is a mix of all good things a pub should be: architecturally interesting and historic with 220 years of history and using the black and red patterned brick that so suits Lewes pubs like the Crown and the Lansdown. Like the Lansdown, it also curves gracefully round the corner it sits on, but enjoys a quieter side street in a more historic location. Its roadside location on a near-traffic-free road means that drinkers spilling out onto the road have unofficially claimed it as the pub's front beer garden, as well as their stadium for the pub's range of quirky pub events. In previous centuries however, complaints were made about the rowdy nature of the Lewes Arms' customers who lurked outside.

An interesting feature: the pub is nestled into the original motte (mound) of an abutting Norman castle; the Lewes Arms is actually next to the original of two mottes, Brack Mount, part of which one year ended up even closer to the Lewes when a mini-avalanche took place into the pub's rear beer garden after heavy rain. The pub was once known as the 'Brack Mount' by its drinkers, if not officially, and the beer garden at the time actually reached up onto the mound.

The beer garden, like the Rights of Man's (see next), is upstairs behind the pub and is a cosy and social spot today, along with a raised terrace and it might be why the pub was featured in the *Telegraph*'s list of Britain's best pubs. If not, then possibly it could be its reputation for hearty, home-cooked food. The Lewes Arms is made even more special by the unique range of unusual events it hosts, as well as some familiar pastimes such as toad and chess tournaments; it is home to the annual World Pea-Throwing Championship, marbles, a yearly dwyle flunking match (banned for many years), pantomimes and spaniel racing. My favourite thing about the Spaniel racing competition is that the participants don't have to be spaniels. Or even dogs. The requirements are that the entrants have to be 'at least animals, who do not have to be spaniels but must dress like them'. Nor is there any shortage of space in such a compact venue for the indoor variants of these activities, with some of the best function venues in Lewes. The whole of the second floor, can be used as a function room and comes complete with its own stage. Unfortunately these aren't big enough for the activities of the pub's stoolball and mixed netball teams.

Whether it's taking on the mighty Greene King brewery giant, other Lewesians at dwyle flunking or racing spaniels, there is a competitive and cheeky spirit to the Lewes Arms you can't help but like. Even the colour of a feature on the pub's sign has caused debate and disagreement. Not until 1976 was an age-old dispute finally settled as to what colour the lion on the arms shown on the pub sign should actually be. The Lewes lion on the sign was founded about 1300, but in 1903 experts declared that the colour of the lion should be silver. Disagreement followed and in 1976 the pub finally changed its lion to gold, after a ruling by experts thirteen years earlier that this was the true colour. Since then the sign has had a lion resplendent in gold, with blue tongue and talons, with a red eye to match its medieval origins, the accurate coat of arms of the first lords of Lewes.

A lion quite suits the Lewes Arms, not only as it is part of the town's coat of arms, but as the pub has something of a lion heart about it. Whether it is standing up for the rights of loyal Lewes tipplers, or ensuring Lewes' heraldry is correctly portrayed, the Lewes Arms is a pub that likes to get things right.

12. The Rights of Man, High Street

Talking of rights, we now move southward back onto the High Street, which is an area surprisingly devoid of recently renovated pubs apart from Harveys' sole tied pub which is a lively, modern pub in an historic building. This is an area of hotels and large pubs, so those seeking cosier boozers need to head west, up to the Black Horse, Brewers or Pelham, back north or down south to the Lansdown. The ROM was opened on the site of the old Rainbow Tavern to presumably capture the (often American) tourist market who flock to the former county town for its claims as birthplace of the American and French revolutions as well as those who want a town centre pub. It is a surprisingly large pub with many rooms and corridors to the rear, so that those wanting to commemorate the meeting place of Lewes 'bad boy' Thomas Paine (bizarrely in the rival drinking establishment of the White Hart hotel across the road from it), as well as his general association with the town have plenty of space to do so. The White Hart might be where Paine met at the Headstrong Club, but it is far nicer to sit in the 'Rights' and look across at the White Hart than actually drink in its admittedly historic, but neglected and Spartan bar which feels in need of a caring, thoughtful, respectful and comprehensive revamp.

Sitting in the ROM is something you mostly do on high stools or at the bar if you do want to sit in view of Paine's famous claimed birthplace of the American Revolution. Being a narrow pub catering for large

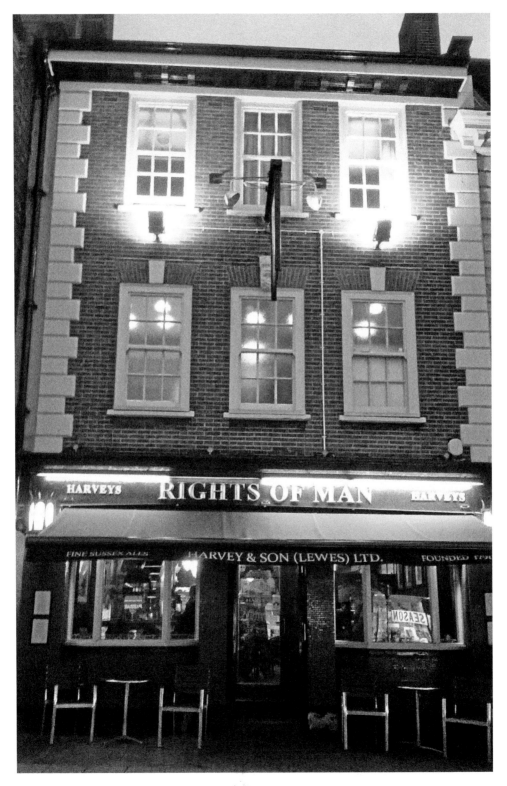

The Rights of Man, a pub about Thomas Paine, to study the meeting place of ...
Thomas Paine.

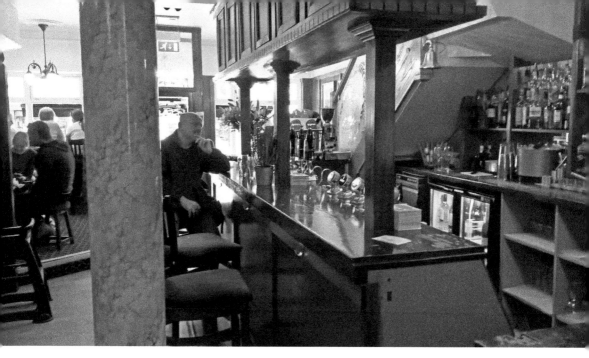

The Rights of Man, as frequented by lead-singer lookalikes of the band 'James'.

numbers of drinkers and eaters, it experiences much 'through-flow' of customers. This means that lower down seatings, such as for younger families, are at a premium, and at busy times you might be better off moving towards the back or upstairs to the terrace. Thomas Paine fans will of course know the pub takes its name from one of his two most famous publications, the other being *Common Sense*. The name change certainly is an example of common sense, after its former names of 'Lincolns' and 'Rainbows' (both of which sound like junior Scout groups) taken respectively from Lincoln's Wine Bar and the Rainbow Tavern. The name 'Rainbow' with its associated colour scheme may also have been seen in recent years as hinting that the pub was a gay bar, which may not have been the direction the owners wanted it to take. Calling a pub after Paine is a great nod to Lewes' important role in the development in the birth of the American and subsequently French revolutions – Paine played a role in both – but it is a shame perhaps that Bull House, which is far older and where Paine actually lived, is not still the 'Bull' as it was in its earliest days – a pub or even a hotel where Paine devotees could imbibe as well as be inspired.

The ROM was originally Bodle's Beer House and existed at least as far back as the 1850s. It was the Rainbow Tavern by at least 1868, which seems an unusual (and very rare) choice of name for the mid-Victorian period, with the reason behind the choice of name now long forgotten. Rebuilt in the 1930s, it kept the same name, but adjusted slightly as 'The Rainbow'. Between 2009 and 2012 it went through its short-lived wine bar phase, perhaps an unlucky choice of timing as the recession hit. Since 2012 it has been owned by Harveys but faces mixed reviews, some people loving its beer, others being less complimentary. The feedback initially on its interior decor was also mixed, but then some Lewesians seem to hate any change to their pubs. It has enough rooms that drinkers have a choice of how modern they want their decor, and outdoor-loving-types have the splendid and large upstairs beer terrace, which is Lewes' only one to have a direct view up at the barbican gate of the castle, making you want to explore the castle after a pint.

The choice of pints is a hard task, with a full range of Harveys on offer as you would expect from a Harveys pub in Lewes' premier location. The barman on my last visit was also incredibly helpful and allowed trials of the different types, along with his recommendations, which were honest, frank and very insightful. Along with the wonderful Martyrs' Bar at the rear of the pub, this all adds up to the fact that the Rights of Man is a great pub with much to offer. It is exciting to have a pub that invites you to explore it in full, providing you with so many different spots to eat or drink depending on your mood. All dead in the centre of town, with a view of a historic spot that changed the world.

13. The Shelleys, High Street

The Shelleys is actually another hotel, but its bar deserves a mention and it also merits inclusion due to its age; it is also another of Lewes' lost inns, the Vine. Its bar today is worthy of a drink on perhaps the most special of occasions as it is in a stunning country house hotel, with an accompanying à la carte restaurant and beautiful gardens of a size you wouldn't expect on the historic high street of Lewes. You move from the hustle and bustle of what was once one of Sussex's busiest highways into tranquillity in a seventeenth-century, family-run establishment. Should you need to avoid a long journey home afterwards you have the option of one of nineteen luxury boutique rooms, all en suite and each designed and decorated to reflect the hotel's Georgian origin.

It is hard to get many older buildings in Lewes than The Shelleys where you can eat or drink (unless you take an impromptu picnic up to the castle). Dating back to the 1520s, The Shelleys, a Grade II-listed

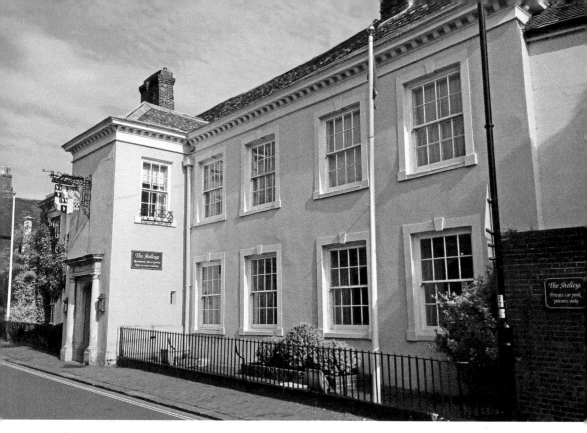

Above: The Shelleys (plural!) hotel, once the Vine.

Below: The Shelleys hotel sign.

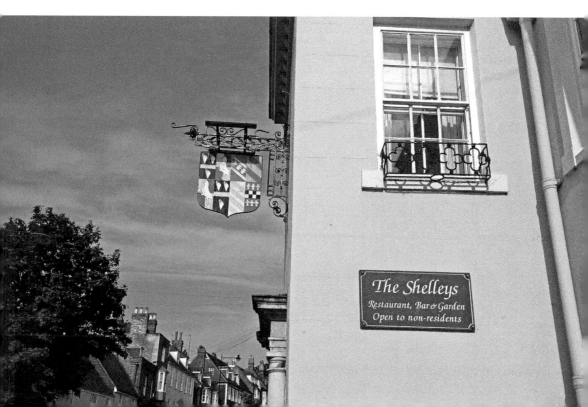

building, comprises the oldest part of the building that was originally
an inn. Should you want to see the original pub sign then a short trek is
needed to Anne of Cleves House Museum where it has been preserved.
Another relic of the building's days as an inn is the date '1577' carved
into the stone porch, as well as the initials of the landlord of the time,
Thomas Pelland. It could well have ended up as a second or alternative
Dorset Arms because, in 1590, the building was sold to the 4th Earl
of Dorset but he converted the inn into a manor house, selling it to
Henry Shelley in 1663, from whom it takes its present name.

The Shelleys did indeed live there for some two centuries, so the hotel
does indeed perhaps deserve a name reflecting the family that owned
it for the longest continuous period in its history. By the lack of an
apostrophe, it appears the hotel celebrates its link to *all* these Shelleys,
and especially capitalises on the Sussex links of its most celebrated
member. Henry Shelley was a relation of the celebrated poet, Percy
Bysshe Shelley. Should punctuation terrorists moan the lack of an
apostrophe, or indeed a focus on just one Shelley then they can find
one in the name of the award-winning Apostrophe Restaurant or on the
brick-paved terrace overlooking the gardens. Lewes could, if this catches
on, start a new trend in punctuation-themed eating establishments.
You can just see the ladies who lunch saying to each other now, 'Well,
Cynthia, I am very partial to the frittatas at *Semi-Colons*, but you really
must try the canapés at *Exclamation Marks*, they're simply divine.'

The literary reference in the restaurant's name may instead refer to
a patron of words, Dr Samuel Johnson. The renowned Dr Johnson
could also have started the genre of child-behaviour-improvement-
management books centuries before they arrived with his different
method of dealing with a challenging child. The author of the English
language's first ever dictionary dealt with a loquacious child who
wouldn't stop chattering by lifting the loud little one up into a cherry
tree in the gardens of the Vine (as it was then) and simply leaving her
there. What would Supernanny say?

Just as spellings in a dictionary may change over time, so have the uses
and wording of the Vine, even after its name changed to the Shelleys.
The Shelley family sold the house in 1854, after which it saw numerous
and far more rapidly changing ownership than for the two centuries
before, even becoming flats for a while until the First World War when
the house was used as a military hospital for officers. The Heriot

family, its owners in 1932, decided to convert it back to a hotel and named it Shelleys Hotel. It then remained privately owned until 1972, when it was purchased by a private group and then, in 1977, ownership was transferred to Mount Charlotte Investments, based in Leeds. The group owned twenty-five hotels at the time, two nightclubs and were manufacturers of wine, spirits and liqueurs. It seemed to be the location for wealthy foreign visitors to Lewes as managing director at the time Robert Peel explained: 'It [gives] a good impression and [is] typical of how many foreigners [imagine] the English hotel.' Mount Charlotte thankfully, despite their financial clout, made no drastic renovations to the hotel in the decade that taste forgot, as it has been called. Peel explained: 'We like the character of Shelleys and want to keep it exactly as it is. I am a great believer in this hotel and its potential.'

Following this period of corporate ownership, The Shelleys returned to private ownership in 2003 and several years later, the name of the hotel was changed from Shelleys Hotel to just The Shelleys. The hotel had now come almost full circle, with not just its name returning to its original when first a hotel in the seventeenth century, but the building being owned by one family once more. Peter and Sylvie Pattenden have been the owners since then, managing Lewes' most expensive hotel from France.

The age of the property means it has some interesting quirks that are only achieved with venerable buildings. It is worth investigating the door to Room 6 which, on approach, one sees that the door is leaning to quite a degree. This may of course be exacerbated should you tackle the Shelleys extensive wine list to any degree. Another quirk is the claim that the hotel has not just one but four ghosts, even outstripping the Crown in its apparent need for a ghostbuster and having two ghosts in one room alone. During 1978 a QC staying in Room 26, while dealing with a case at Lewes Crown Court, decided to stay elsewhere after his bed was reportedly levitated three inches above the floor in the course of the night. Guests also experienced other poltergeist activity that year, such as ashtrays, clothes hangers and clothes being moved around the room by forces unseen. These experiences may be linked to the sad case of the man who also stayed in the room, but four decades earlier, in the 1930s. He departed at speed the following morning after his stay, so distressed that he left his clothes behind, and gassed himself to death at a nearby relative's house. Quite why he didn't stay with them on the previous evening is anybody's guess but at least it means that the room wasn't the site of a suicide itself.

Should you prefer your ghosts to be of a Civil War vintage, then hope that you witness the same visitation as the manager of the hotel, David Nicholas, who told John Eccles of the *Sussex Express* that the ghost of a Cavalier had been seen near the staircase of the sixteenth-century site of the building. The most regular appearance, however, seems to be in one of the upper corridors of the hotel where the phantom of an old lady in a blue and white dress has popped up more than once. She been witnessed by both members of the staff and occasional guests.

14. The Pelham Arms, St Anne's Hill

As we have seen, Lewes has many pubs celebrating its connections with wealthy, landed and aristocratic patrons of the town. However, there is, interestingly, no De Warenne Arms, after the town's Norman landowner and castle-builder. Nor is there any record of there ever having been one.

As we journey west up the northern side of Lewes' main thoroughfare, as the High Street merges into St Anne's Hill, the Pelham Arms is no exception, also celebrating another landed family who lived in the town. Built in Stuart times, around 1640, and originally owned by the Duke of Newcastle, this pub and restaurant is unsurprisingly, Grade II-listed. It is named after the Pelham family, major Sussex landowners who resided at Stanmer House in Brighton. The Duke of Newcastle's name was Thomas Pelham, and he also happened to be prime minister, so the Pelham is Lewes' only pub named after a former premier. Thirty years older than the Crown, it contests the title of oldest pub in Lewes, even older than the Dorset in Cliffe.

Dogs are welcome in the bar areas, as are children (until 8 p.m.) which befits the fact that the pub was for a while called the Dog. Other creatures of the equine variety were also much in discussion at the Pelham for many years after the pub was sold to a Richard Williams in 1799. He was clerk to the Lewes racecourse as well as the pub's landlord and the Pelham subsequently became the meeting place of Lewes' racing fraternity from that point, helped by its siting near the now-abandoned racecourse. The horsey theme continued at the Pelham during the nineteenth century with a retired jockey, Thomas Reed, becoming landlord. Reed attracted other racing pundits and fans and one of his most famous customers was the nineteenth century's most famous jockey, Fred Archer. Horsemeat

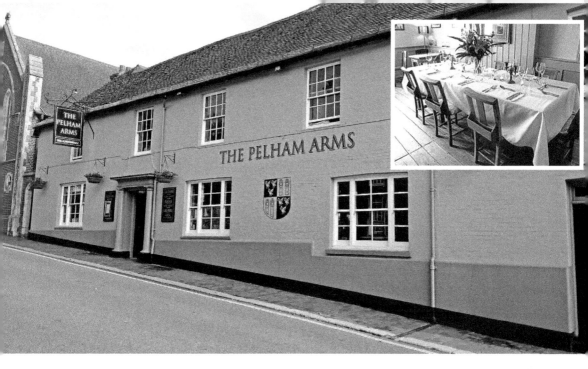

Above: The Pelham Arms, 2016, the first hostelry in Lewes to use the Pelham name but, confusingly, not the last. *Inset*: The pub's interior.

Right: The Pelham Arms sign.

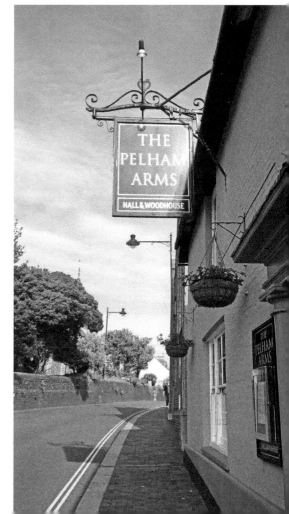

remains, unsurprisingly, off the menu to this day. What is on the menu is smoked meat, however. The Pelham has taken the unique step in Lewes in having its own smokehouse so customers can now try smoked salt beef, pork belly, turkey breast and chicken wings. While you munch on a wing, you can listen to hot vintage Gypsy Swing, the live music of choice in the pub every first Thursday in the month.

The Pelham has not only survived the loss of the nearby racecourse in 1964 but a planned demolition as part of extensive redevelopment in the area back in the same decade. Thankfully the Friends of Lewes were able to beat the builders and Lewes' western sector is still blessed with an architecturally appreciated building as well as the friendly and full-of-character inn that is the Pelham.

15. The Black Horse, Western Road

Moving westward and further uphill from the High Street into Western Road, the Black Horse also controversially decided not to stock Harveys back in the early 2000s but somehow escaped the wrath incurred when Greene King did the same at the Lewes Arms. Today it specialises in gin, with a full menu of the ruin of mothers. It once had bed and breakfast available, but seems to focus now on its food instead. Its wooden decor and revamp of the last decade make it a tidy and warm pub that you can visit to escape the throngs of tourists and spend time choosing your choice of pub game to play. Other sporting challenges took place near the Black Horse in the nineteenth century when, like the Pelham, it also benefited from its proximity to the racecourse. Racehorse trainers were apparently even busy in the neighbouring stables but the pub today, with a charming range of old photos, celebrates other old pubs more than its racing heritage, which is where it gets its name from – a black horse called Waxy that was famous in the 1790s. The pub opened less than two decades after Waxy won the Derby in 1793. The first owner of the pub, Richard Goddard, who had run the nearby (and since demolished) Running Horse, opened the pub in 1809 and thankfully decided not to call it the Waxy Tavern, which would have sounded rather odd and slightly unappealing, with potential punters being reminded of earwax.

Not only was the pub named after a horse, but on one occasion it almost ended up serving them drinks too. During the Napoleonic Wars, when, like many Lewes establishments with boarding, Royal Artillery officers were staying in its rooms, along with their horses in the stables

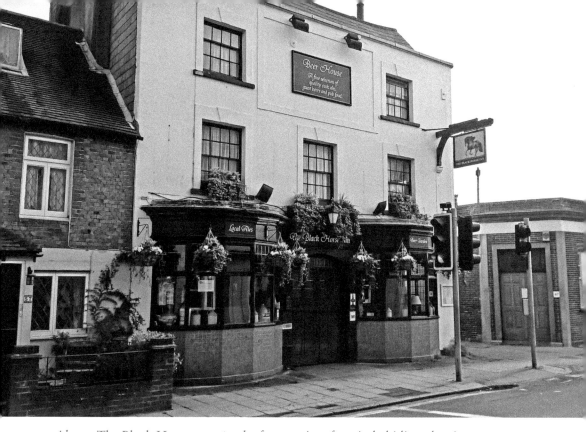

Above: The Black Horse, 2016 – the former site of a windy hiding place?

Below: The Black Horse, the ground-floor entrance and sign.

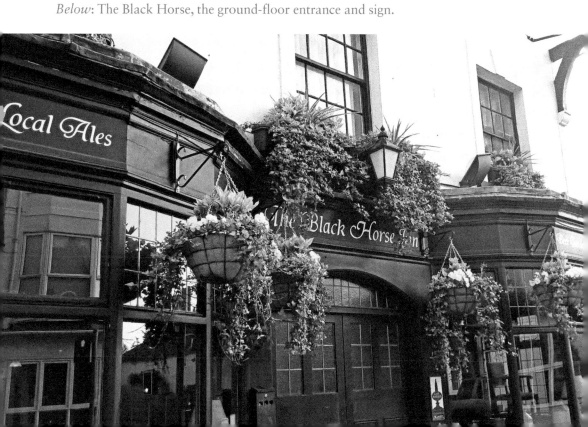

behind. Two of the horses, after a scare, knocked down a wall and then crashed through the rear entrance to the pub. The narrow hallway prevented them getting to the bar and, helped by a brave customer, they were led through the pub and out the front entrance (the corridor presumably being too small to turn around in and return out the back). There was once an earlier Black Horse pub, but the location of this is unknown, although it has been speculated that it was in the Station Street area.

Richard Goddard could have chosen an earlier and more historical, if not necessarily corroborated, event for the name of the pub should he not have decided to have a second horse-named pub. The site of the pub, or at least its vicinity, was the location according to legend of the hiding place of Richard, Duke of Gloucester, after the king's forces had been routed at the Battle of Lewes on 14 May 1264. Richard, Henry III's brother, used the mill to hide, barricading the door from inside until his surrender to the rebel leader, Sir Henry Bevis, who was reputedly a giant of a man. He was forced to endure a number of taunts from Simon de Montfort's men during his refuge, such as 'thou wicked miller' and 'thou unlucky master of the mill'. Those medieval taunts don't quite seem as cutting today, somehow, but they could provide a more memorable and historically ancient pub name. Who's for a pint in the Wicked Miller?

16. The Tally Ho, Baxter Road, Landport

Still north of the High Street, our most northerly pub still within the boundaries of Lewes is the Tally Ho pub situated on the outskirts of the main town on the edge of the Landport housing estate. It is more of a locals' pub than most of the Lewes pubs, as its distance from the town centre makes it an unlikely destination for tourists or visitors. It can be used as part of a 'Footie Route' if you want the challenge of watching the first half of a match on your way into Lewes from the north, and then catch the second half in the Elly. As the latter can show more than one match simultaneously, this is a real possibility.

The pub was the last to be built from scratch in Lewes, as part of the construction of the Landport estate, not something that often happens with the construction of new housing developments today, for some reason. It was constructed partially as a replacement to the White Lion in Westgate Street, which was demolished in 1939 as part of the slum clearance next to the town walls. The Tally Ho's licence was issued to

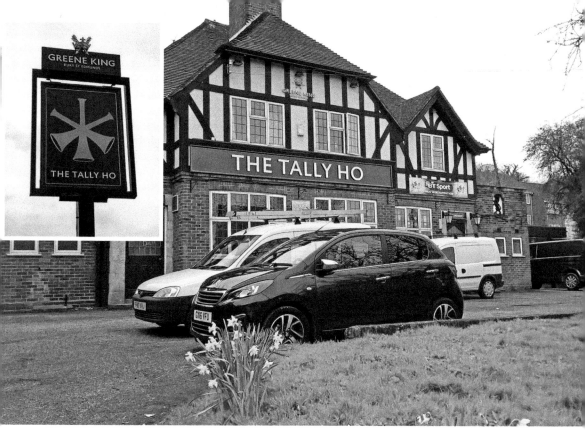

Above: The Tally Ho, 2016 – the carpark makes the pub look busier than it is.
Inset: The pub sign.

Below: The Tally Ho on a quiet Saturday lunchtime.

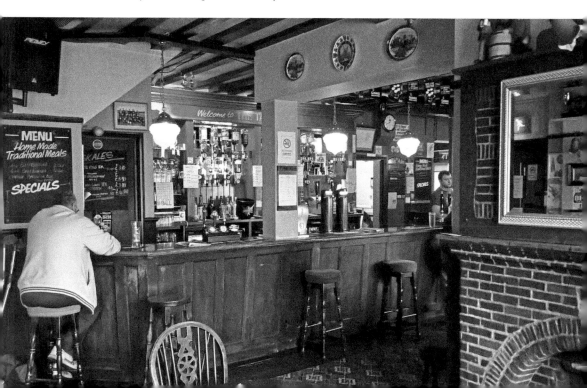

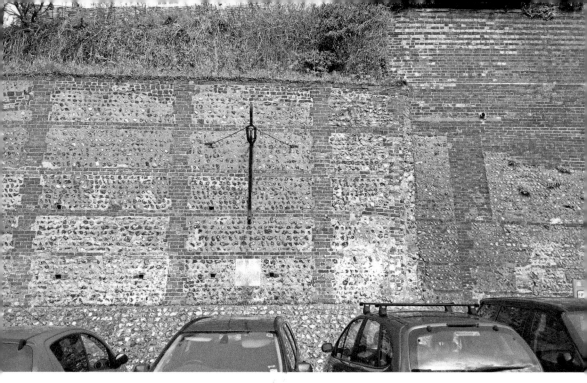

The memorial to the White Lion, the pub the Tally Ho replaced.

replace that lost to Beard's Brewery at the White Lion, who were behind the Tally Ho's construction. It is possible that the White Lion, today commemorated by a plaque on the town walls and unfortunately just a raggedy car park, was something the authorities were glad to demolish because of a gruesome past: the last landlord and landlady used the pub oven to gas themselves to death in 1931. The White Lion was not too dissimilar to the Lewes Arms or the Lansdown in its age or build, except for it was in the middle of a terrace, not curving round a corner.

The Tally Ho's name alludes to the fact that its northerly aspect in the town means it looks out to the rolling Sussex countryside and its foxhunts, of course legal at the time. This was an aspirational class move for the Landport Estate and its pub, which would include many council house tenants, not usually themselves hunt groupies. The name of the pub may have no links to its older sister pub, but it does have a clue in terms of the 'Lion rampant' built into its wall, next to the entrance. Unfortunately, the lion has been painted black. It is strange to think that rather than foxhunters, the shout of 'Tally ho!' would have been called instead by Battle of Britain fighter pilots having sighted the enemy in the skies above Lewes just two years after it was built. Perhaps a better name today for the pub might be the Battle of Lewes, the Henry III or the Simon de Montfort, as although local street names commemorate the nearby battle of 1264, there is no pub in Lewes named after this clash in an early English Civil War which led, some argue, to the birth of Parliament in this country.

Inside today, this Greene King pub has a roomy feel, with friendly bar staff and a lovely landlady of the type pubs often sadly lack these days, with hints of Ealing Comedies and Peggy Mitchell all rolled into one. The thirties architecture has come into its own and has been mostly well preserved, meaning that the Tally Ho is an underappreciated building that would benefit from greater access from the main road and a thoughtful revamp. It has a Greene King sign on the main road which is a bit of a tease, as there is no easy access to the pub from the road, despite the appearance of what looks like a slip road. The Tally Ho doesn't benefit from Lewes' best views, heritage or location, so it needs to perhaps offer more if it is to survive and not become another Tesco Express. Online reviews have mentioned its poor reputation in the past and how its limited clientele can feel quite intimidating to newcomers; it did seem to be a bit of a lads-only pub when I last visited. However, reviews relate that it has a brilliant atmosphere during big sporting events.

So, a pub named after a bloodsport still focuses as sport over eighty years later (though thankfully not of the cruel type).

Chapter Three

Lewes – South Side and South of the High Street

17. The Brewers Arms, High Street

There are far fewer pubs on the south side of Lewes and its High Street, and the Brewers is the only actual standalone pub on the southern side of the High Street itself, the only other place selling ale being the White Hart Hotel. This means that it has one of the better, rare views of the Ouse Valley that 'South Side' hostelries tend to have. The Brewers is also a rarity in this day and age as a family-run pub that is also a free house, owned by the Griffin family since 1994, and who celebrated their twentieth anniversary as landlord by temporarily reducing prices in 2014 to 1994 prices. The pub has much else to celebrate as the proud winners of Pub of the Year in the Brighton and South Downs CAMRA region 2015 and have been on the CAMRA 'Ale Trail' for many years. This is no flash in the pan, either: they have been either runner-up or pub of the year for the CAMRA Brighton and South Downs region since 2011.

It is in an enviable location for those visiting the castle, as it's the nearest pub on the High Street to William de Warenne's Norman headquarters. The front bar of the Brewers is handy for watching those visiting the castle, or indeed just people-watching in Lewes' main road, in a peaceful, music-free setting. The walls are adorned with historic photographs of Lewes, as well as the original building plans for the pub, and a list of

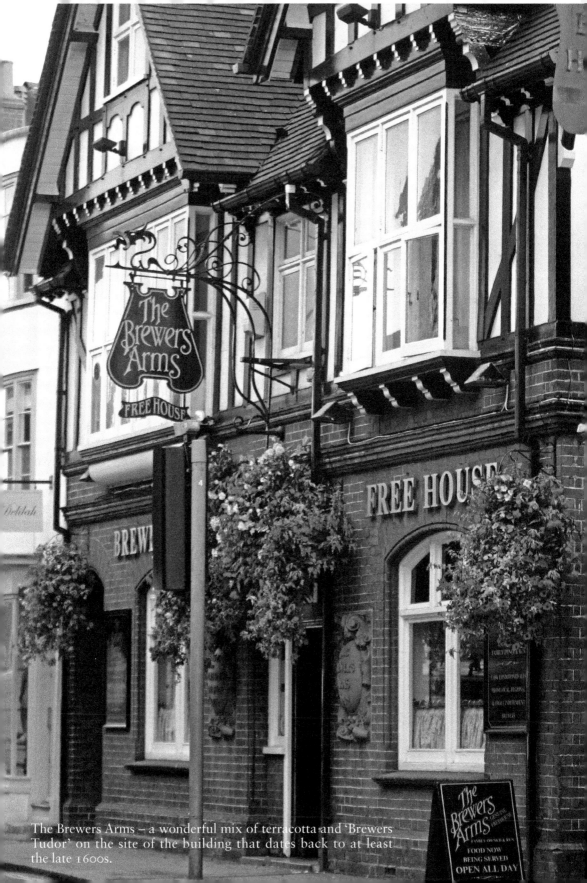

The Brewers Arms – a wonderful mix of terracotta and 'Brewers Tudor' on the site of the building that dates back to at least the late 1600s.

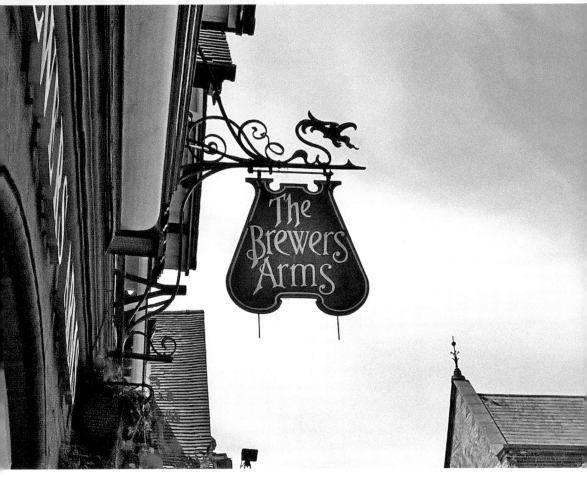

Above: The Brewers Arms pub sign.

Below: Bull House, once the Bull Inn (and home of Thomas Paine); its conversion to private dwelling is perhaps why the Brewers was needed.

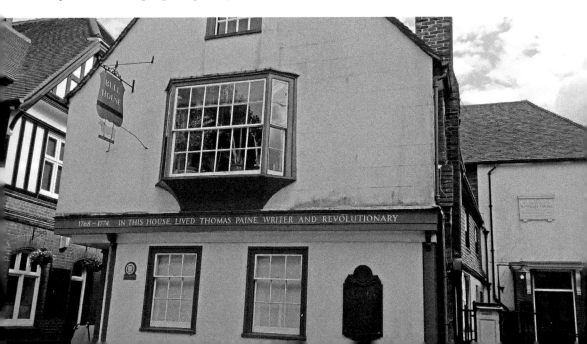

licensees from 1744 when the building on site was called The Ship. The back bar is a very different beast, with Sky TV, pool, darts, a jukebox, free WiFi and the chance for a lively game of Toad. Continuing through and you enter a suntrap of a patio garden, something central Lewes seems to do so well to make up for its lack of green space.

Though the present structure dates from 1906, a tavern has graced this spot since the sixteenth century. There has been a public house on this site since the seventeenth century. It would have been just inside the Westgate wall of the town since at least 1687 and by 1696 it was not just a pub, but comprised a messuage, brewhouse, slaughterhouse and stables. It seems to have to have become a pub when the Bull Inn next door became a private house. It went through a rapid period of three name changes: until 1744 it was known as the Red Lion, then briefly The Ship. This name may seem a little peculiar what with it being on a hilltop and far away from Lewes' shipbuilding yard (which reached its peak later in the early 1800s anyway), but it is thought perhaps to be more biblical and metaphorical in its origin rather than a nautical reference. The name of the Ship in this case symbolised Noah's Ark as a place of shelter. The churchwardens of St Michael's, opposite the pub, used to hold their parish meetings here and perhaps sought its comforts as a refuge from their duties. Or parishoners. It is not impossible that they influenced the name change. St Michael's was a lively place of worship before the Reformation, with dinners, celebrations and drinking of church ales, so perhaps the wardens of the 1700s missed what their counterparts of two centuries before had been allowed to do in the church.

From a reference to one type of liquid, sea or river water, to another. The pub then changed its name to reflect someone who made his living doing something totally different with water. The wonderfully named Obediah Elliot, a brewer in Fisher Street who already owned the building, changed the name to glorify his trade in 1769, which it has remained ever since, even during the 1905–06 almost total rebuild. The pub does technically deserve its name of the 'Brewers' (plural) Arms as it was also owned back in 1696 by the wonderfully named Robert Rossum, who sold it in that year for £120.

The 1905–06 rebuild was undertaken by much-esteemed brewers Page & Overton of the Shirley Brewery in Croydon and is an early example of what later hit its peak the 1930s as 'Brewer's Tudor'. Their impressive terracotta signs reflect the trend of the time in buildings using this material from the 1880s, alongside red brick, which increased with the popularity of the buildings of leading Victorian architect Alfred Waterhouse, whose premier building locally must be the Hilton Brighton Metropole (as it is now called), built in 1890. Visitors can still see the delicate Page & Overton carvings in terracotta either side of the front door. That brewery, taken over in 1929 and demolished in 1972, is still also commemorated by the etchings in the front glass windows which have thankfully survived. One thing that doesn't seem to have continued into the twenty-first century is whatever used to reputedly haunt the pub. The current owners say they've never had any evidence of spooky goings-on in their twenty-two years of running the pub, despite the alleged fact that a resident was apparently strangled in an upstairs bedroom many years ago. This may have been by the strangler's own hand: the only record of such an occurrence was of a soldier in 1804 during the Napoleonic Wars, when the pub's Club Room at the rear was used by local billeted soldiers. The gunner in question was found dangling in his billet and died despite his colleague's attempts to revive him.

Returning to the present and on a more cheerful note, the current owners, Kevin and Joan Griffin, bought the pub in 1994 and today run it together with their son Liam, daughter Kathy and son-in-law Paul Simmonds. Lewes certainly has pubs where the owners put heart and soul into making their home more than just a place to drink, and the Brewers is, like the Elly, a great example of this. Those entering are given the opportunity for games, chats with interesting regulars, challenges and a sense of belonging, a home from home. The Griffins and Simmonds clan try to make being an extended family member (or 'customer' as they're known in less friendly pubs) of the Brewers like being a member of a lively club, with a full range of activities. As you would expect there are toad competitions inside, along with darts challenges, 'Meet the Brewer' events, talks, quizzes, cake nights, cribbage and outside, inter-pub stoolball championships; the Brewers even hosts its own 'Olympics'. This first took place in 2012 involving a range of games and planned to return again in the summer of 2016. Entrants attending the Brewers' Olympics can save themselves a journey as the events are all in-house classic pub sports: darts, pool, toads, and ring the bull. The only expedition that will mean adjourning into the outside world will be a challenging race up the very steep St Swithun's Terrace behind the pub. Should physical and mental exertion not be your thing, then potential customers will be glad to read that the Brewers recently had its first beer festival where drinkers could try out the challenge of comparing different beers.

Returning for less strenuous activities on their morning visits are the loyal regulars, who Kathy Simmonds fondly admits 'mean everything to us' and you can indeed tell the genuine affection that exists for them, as they have been dubbed the 'Last of the summer wine'. It's not clear if anyone specifically reminds people of Compo, Clegg and Foggy, and hopefully not Nora Batty, but the pub is frequented by no less than John Eccles, mentioned at the start of the book and described as local legend by Kathy the landlady. John has over thirty years' experience at Lewes' *Sussex Express* and despite his huge local knowledge about all aspects of local life, he admits that when it comes to crosswords, he can't do one to save his life. Other excitingly named customers include 'Racy Phil', who has become an 'honorary member of staff', earning the title by meeting and greeting customers, and by knowing what is (or more importantly) should be going on at all times. Should the intellect of John Eccles not be enough for new customers seeking stimulating conversation, then the Brewers even has its own resident polymath, Kitworth, and to fulfill any religious needs of the clientele, the wonderfully named Monsignor Heaven is the pub's 'spiritual leader'. We would not expect anything less of course in a pub that seems to have its roots as a place of escape for church wardens back in the 1700s. Should you wish to read the wit and wisdom of this great group of people, then the Brewers has even published a book of quotes from them and other customers, in aid of St Peter and St James's Hospice, entitled *You're quite sober for a Monday!*

The Brewers seems to have a unique brew of regulars who, according to Kathy are just as friendly and helpful to new arrivals as the staff. Dogs are also welcomed too, as are non-beer drinkers, who will find themselves able to try their hand at the range of wines supplied by local Lewes-based wine emporium, Symposium, further helping local business. Drinkers at the Brewers may cross over from beer to wine but for some there is one line they will never cross. Most regulars will happily cross between the two very different bars, from the quieter front one to the noisier rear one which generally attracts a younger trade, but there are some customers who would never dream of venturing from one to the other. A line Kathy says that the owners will never thankfully cross is to contemplate any major changes to the pub or its layout in future years. 'Good Lord, no!' Kathy explained. The Brewers has brewed up a successful combination of ingredients since the 1600s and long may it stay that way.

18. The Pelham House Hotel, St Andrew's Lane

It would have been nice to have been able to feature the long-lost Dolphin Inn in St Nicholas Lane before we reach the Pelham House Hotel, not to be confused with the Pelham Arms on St Anne's Hill. From all accounts, it was a lovely old pub, another part of the Page & Overton chain and a thriving establishment in the days when the market took place in the High Street. The Pelham House Hotel is very different to what the Dolphin would have been like, but has an interesting lounge bar that makes it a welcome diversion from the High Street taverns for those who don't mind spending a bit more. Again, although not technically a pub as such, I make no apologies for including it as I am a hotel historian as well as a firm advocate of the belief that we should support hotel bars as well as pubs. Hotel bars often get overlooked by locals, and yet can be the most historic of watering holes, as well as often as lively as any boozer. Their clientele is forever changing and they are often a more exciting all-round experience than just a sit in a one-roomed bar with no beer garden or food. For a family with young children, at the price of a pub meal they offer so much more to explore. They can also be great for people-watching. Hotel bars need not necessarily be that more expensive than pub prices, especially with the exorbitant cost of wine these days, but admittedly the Pelham House Hotel is a place for people to treat themselves to. You will pay more than on Lewes High Street and hotels in general can cost half a mortgage more than a Northern Wetherspoons but it is worth it as the building is sumptuous, a beautiful sixteenth-century townhouse hotel, recently exquisitely restored to create a stylish venue, which combines elegance and history. The bar at Pelham House is a light and airy place to relax, with sofas and banquettes and, for those who like to be surrounded by culture while they sip, regularly changing art exhibitions. Pelham House has long been associated with promoting local artists and they feature exhibitions by different artists in the hotel.

You would think that the Pelham House Hotel was one of Lewes' oldest establishments, but it has a long and varied history before it was

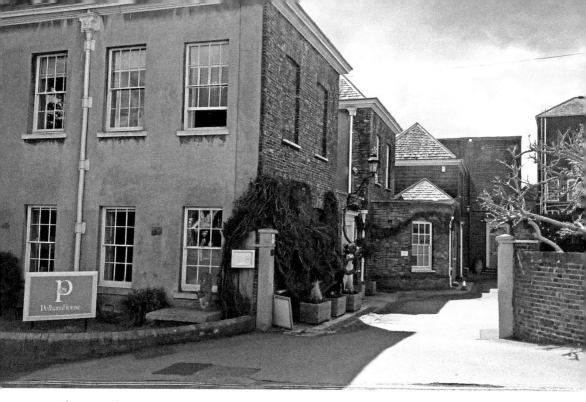

Above: Pelham House Hotel; the original mansion cost an exorbitant £2,000 back in the 1500s.

Below: The bar at the Pelham House Hotel. *Inset*: Pelham House Hotel, 2016, a misnamed but exquisite venue for a special occasion.

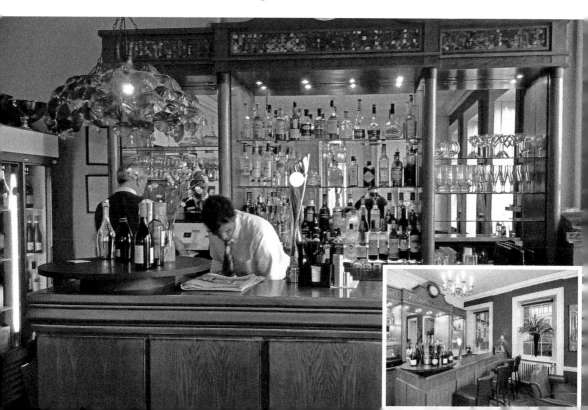

a council building only relatively recently sold off and converted into a hotel by four families who jointly purchased it. Despite the similarity of name with the Pelham Arms pub further west, the council decided to commemorate the name of an owner who refurbished the building rather than the man who built the first mansion on the site. There is a Pelham Hotel that exists as well, but thankfully that is in New Orleans, so visitors should only be confused with two establishments. The building's history goes back to at least 1523 when it was a 'humble dwelling' for John Cotmot, the church warden of St Andrew's Church. He lived there until 1563 when George Goring, who was not only a landowner but one of Lewes' two MPs and a lawyer, purchased the land, deciding to replace Cotmot's original building with a stone-built mansion, costing the princely sum of £2,000. This extravagant amount reflected Goring's lack of financial prudence and he died intestate in 1594, owing the Crown £20,000 but his building gives us the outline of the current hotel. Despite Goring Senior's debts, the family managed to keep hold of the house and eventually pass it down to Goring's grandson, another George. George Goring III made a good decision to become a Lewes MP like his grandfather, but a bad decision to financially and otherwise support the Royalists during the Civil War, which cost him his estates, which he was forced to sell.

Goring would have been pained to sell his house to its next owner, Peter Courthope, who was a Parliamentarian and who also picked up the estate linked to the house, barns, stables, outbuildings , gardens, orchards and other parcels of land in the town in the year of Charles I's death in 1649. Courthope sealed the deal at a bargain £500, £1,500 less than Goring's grandfather paid just to build the house. The Pelhams, who the hotel today is named after, purchased the house off Courthope in 1653. The powerful Pelhams were to beat the Gorings for length of tenure in the house, with five different Pelhams (two of whom were also MPs), two Henrys and three Thomases. Three of these were MP for Lewes continually between 1695 and 1743. It is believed the house was remodelled from an Elizabethan mansion into its current Classical style by Thomas Pelham, who bought it in 1725.

After 1806, the house passed from the Pelhams to a large number of different owners including wine merchant William Campion and his descendants, attorney John E. Fullager, Brighton brewer William Robins, magistrate John Ingham Blencowe, spinster Margaret Sikes Duval and stockbroker William Taylor Banks. Banks bought it for £3,580 – still less than £2,000 more than the cost of constructing the original Elizabethan mansion, demonstrating how magnificent that original house must have been. The last owner before it was converted into its current status of hotel was East Sussex County Council, who purchased it for £7,500 when they needed more administrative offices in the town. The council further extended the property so that it also had a council chamber, committee rooms, offices and a storeroom. This was the status quo until 2004. Since then, as well as its delightful airy bar, you can stay in one of its rooms, have lunch, explore the gardens or hold your conference there. It seems fitting that as one of Lewes' oldest pubs became its Town Hall, another civil building became one of Lewes' most prestigious spots for wining and dining. It would have been nice if this hotel perhaps avoided confusion and commemorated another Lewes family in its name, such as the Gorings who built the original mansion or even John Cotmot who first raised a building on this site.

19. The White Hart, High Street

The White Hart, dating back to 1579, was once one of the town houses also owned by the rich and influential Pelham family and was constructed in a timber frame, which has long been covered over by stucco to give it its impressive grand frontage. It takes its name from the white hart on local medieval landowner John of Gaunt's coat of arms. As he owned much land across Sussex it makes it quite a common name for pubs and hotels in the county. It has expanded rapidly since the 1980s when purchased by businessman Cliff Ayris. In 1988, when he took over the ancient coaching inn, it had thirty bedrooms, but by 2002 it had fifty-three, all of which were en suite. It now has three function rooms, two lounges, a coffee shop, Lewes' premier health and fitness suite and even a snack bar. That's not all, however: it also boasts a dance studio, beauty clinic, gym, sauna and solarium and indoor swimming pool. Despite all this, it still retains its heritage as one of Lewes' oldest hostelries, and has a businesslike air, being or having been one of the town's meeting places for its many groups and clubs, whether the Sailing Club, Masons, Rotary, Tennis Club, Bowls, Trout Fishing Club, Lions or Round Table. It is no wonder it could say back at the turn of the century that over 4,000 people every week came through its doors for one reason or another. A century before, early automobiles of the rich

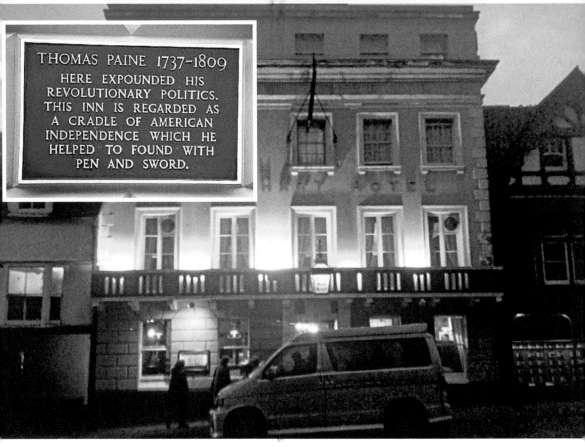

THOMAS PAINE 1737-1809
HERE EXPOUNDED HIS
REVOLUTIONARY POLITICS.
THIS INN IS REGARDED AS
A CRADLE OF AMERICAN
INDEPENDENCE WHICH HE
HELPED TO FOUND WITH
PEN AND SWORD.

Above: White Hart Hotel: the front is grand but the inside is much in need of refurbishment. *Inset*: The sign commemorating Thomas Paine's time in debate at the Headstrong Club.

Below: White Hart Hotel, disappointing for such an historic and important Lewes landmark.

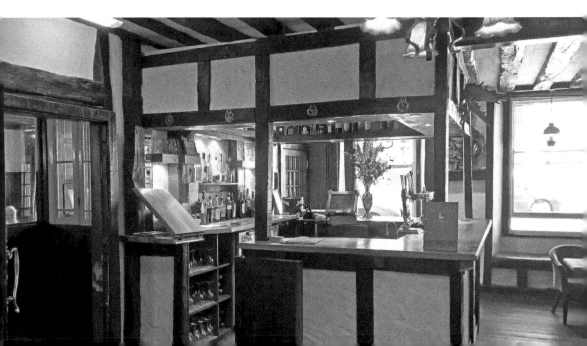

and famous would be parked outside, their drivers imbibing in the more humble Unicorn Inn next door, which is today unfortunately only a shop and yet another lost Lewes inn.

One set of meetings at the hotel that changed the world were those involving future writer and revolutionary Thomas Paine. Living and working down the High Street at Bull House as a revenue official, it is said to be here, at the legendary Headstrong Club, that Paine proclaimed his revolutionary beliefs that would evolve eventually into the publications *Rights of Man* and *Common Sense* that helped spark both the American and French revolutions. It is amazing to think that a meeting in a Lewes hotel changed the world and it is apt that the pub-facing hotel should also celebrate Paine's work. As comedian Mark Steel said in his book, *Mark Steel's In Town*, Paine's hometown of Thetford would only put up a statue to him if it had the word 'traitor' emblazoned upon it. It says much about the unique and radical nature of Lewes that the White Hart once had a cardboard cutout of Paine inviting you for lunch, a pub celebrating a book that turned people against Britain and even a beer named after him brewed by Harveys.

The small front hotel bar is open to non-residents but feels in need of careful renovation to best show off the marvellous oak beams, fireplaces and floorboards. It doesn't feel as if the hotel is making the most of the historic building, nor is it evoking the status it once held as the town's most upmarket hotel. It would be good if the experience one gets in going to the bar in the White Hart matched the level of the hotel's historic significance or its past glories.

20. The Royal Oak, Station Street

Like the Crown, and the bar of the White Hart, the Royal Oak's best days seem at present to be in the past and is much in need of some TLC. This is a shame as it is in an historic building, but its wide windows and top floor are latter architectural additions which seem to have been crudely beaten into the building without a great deal of thought. The top floor looks as though someone has just glued it on. It was a much grander place in past years, with its exquisite assembly room the meeting place of many of Lewes' important clubs. The assembly room can confuse as it sticks out over the premises to the south of the pub. It is also rumoured to be heavily haunted, which seems to be the case with pubs near the site of the martyrs' deaths, like the Crown.

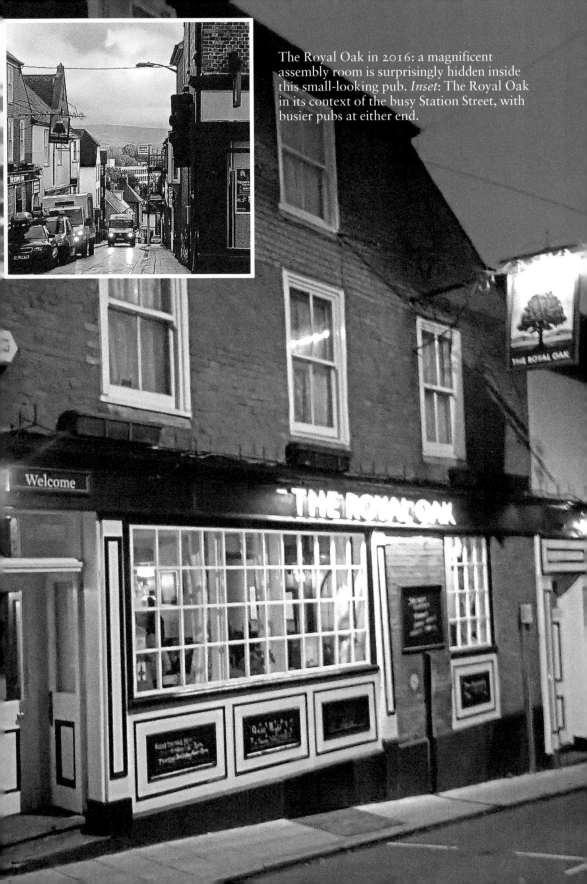

The Royal Oak in 2016: a magnificent assembly room is surprisingly hidden inside this small-looking pub. *Inset*: The Royal Oak in its context of the busy Station Street, with busier pubs at either end.

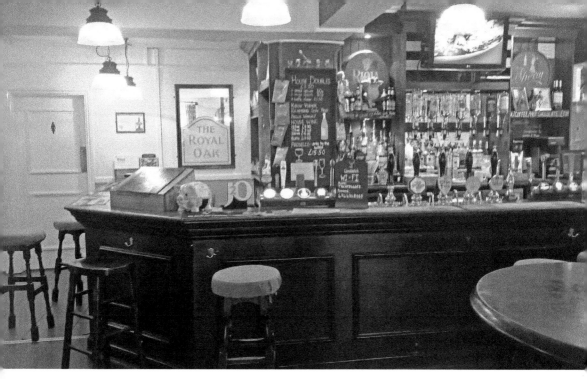

The Royal Oak on a quiet Saturday afternoon.

Today the Oak seems unsure who its clientele is – there wasn't much in the way of locals or regulars there on my last visit, or visitors, shoppers and certainly not any businessfolk or the real ale crowd. It seems to be devoid of an USP and is a little downmarket in what is a very pretty and upmarket town. Its position doesn't help either, sandwiched in between bigger and bouncier pubs at the top of Station Street and the lively Lansdown at the bottom, ready to pick up the first of the incoming or outgoing railway trade. The beers are its one positive feature as it doesn't seem to be known for (or even selling when I visited) its food. The Oak is a great building and once had a large brewery behind it, but it needs to work out its future direction and what makes it different to other drinking spots if it is to survive. It may also not be helping itself by possibly alienating Harveys diehards who remember Greene King's fiasco of 2006 and by its not stocking Harveys either.

Perhaps the Oak could use its past to inspire its present and future. Originally the White Horse and in existence since at least the late 1700s, the pub was bought in 1819 by John Pendrill, who used the financial annuity his forebears had received for assisting Charles II flee to safety in 1651. Commemorating this family link to that king-to-be in hiding, he changed the pub's name to the famous 'Royal Oak' in which Charles supposedly hid from the Parliamentarians. This is why it is a shame that the pub's sign shows the wrong Charles, that of the father of Charles II, Charles I, who had been dead for over a year by the time of the escapade in the tree. The nationwide renaming of pubs long after this event was still very common at the time, either due to Charles's treetop hiding place, or even after Royal Navy ships bearing the same name. Numerous pubs claim to have been places where Charles II passed or stayed at in his escape from the Battle of Worcester, but Lewes' Oak can't make this claim as Charles's most westerly stop was the George Inn in West Street, Brighton, 7 miles away. Pendrill, or his family's assistance in the 'Great Escape' as it is known, might make a good new name for the pub or a focus around it. If this isn't to Greene King's taste, the first registered owner of the White Horse would have been black, in terms of coal dirt – he was a coal merchant who sold coal from the pub. This profession may be another focus for a rename, although it is unlikely that another colour reference to Charles II which causes pubs to be called the Black Boy (Charles's nickname as a child) would find favour these days. An easier theme to rebrand the pub might be its historic association with cricket in Lewes, a town where some of the earliest cricket was e played in this country. Not only did the Oak host, in 1831, the meeting that witnessed the formation of Lewes Priory Cricket Club but supplied its food needs for many years. This could be the most profitable direction for the pub; or once again trying to establish itself as the premier meeting venue in Lewes. At the moment even some of the most knowledgeable of Lewes citizens don't know just what a fantastic and historic gem they have in the Oak's assembly room. Nor is the pub making as much use of it as it could. Like the Crown, the Oak has the potential to become once more not just a great Lewes institution but a great drinkers' and foodies' venue.

21. Lansdown Arms, Station Street

The Lansdown has the feel of a small successful pub – just the right amount of cosiness, a great location as the gateway pub to Lewes by rail and friendly staff. The beers are grown-up and Max the manager gets to know newcomers quickly. It started its life off in 1827 before the main railway terminus, becoming unofficially known as the 'Railway', although there already was 'The Railway' near the old station and a 'New Station Inn' across the road from the Lansdown (since demolished). The

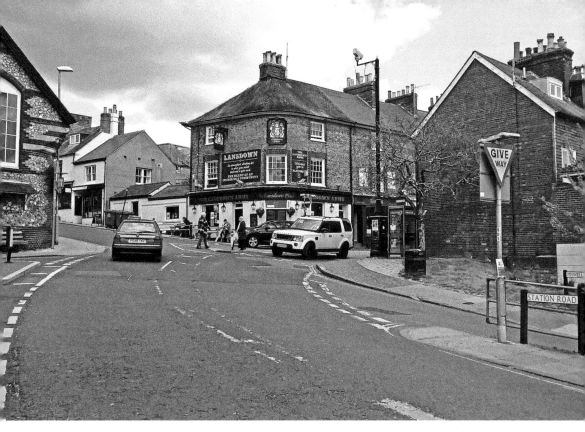

Above: The Lansdown, well placed on the corner of a vibrant part of Lewes, night or day.

Below: The bar at the Lansdown.

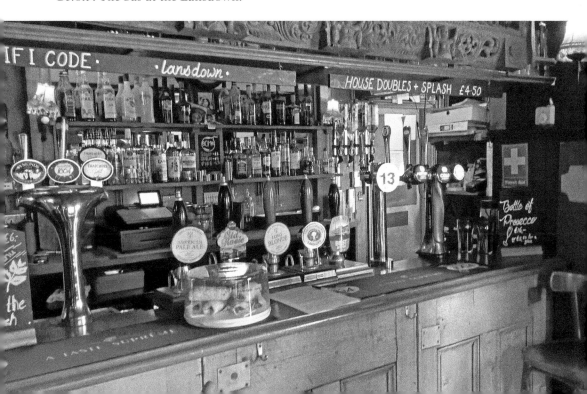

mid-1800s must have been confusing times. The Lansdown saw off the last of its railway-named contenders in the 1960s when the 'Old' Station Inn (as the original 'Railway' came to be known) was demolished, but not before a punch-up between two of the landlords in the 1800s. Still today it is nicknamed 'Platform 6' in reference to its proximity to the station and captures the thirsty end-of-day commuter crowd or the masses off to football wanting a last non-Amex-sold pint or a decent burger.

When an Enterprise Inn, the Lansdown was temporarily the 'White Star Inn' from 2001 for a few years after new landlord Marcus Warland decided he wanted a pub that would house his extensive collection of cruise ship memorabilia. The pub had been quite rough before that, as Warland said, 'not what Lewes needed.' After being closed down, Warland reopened it as a real ale and non-sports pub to change the clientele to that of a more amicable nature. Music became less abrasive and intrusive and its ale sales increased, with the pub making its way into the CAMRA guides, probably due to Warland's membership of the Guild of Master Cellarmen. Visitors and singers off to Glyndebourne also would frequent the pub on their way to the opera and other events as its reputation changed, obviously appreciating the many pictures of White Star liners and other memorabilia the pub displayed, much of which was passed down to Marcus Warland from his grandfather who had worked for the Cunard line. However, ultimately it seems that the clientele weren't too fussed about nauticalia and Warland got too choosy about the clientele, as too many people weren't allowed to 'board'. He only lasted two years as owner.

Today the ale sales are still going strong in the Lansdown with high-quality Timothy Taylor a must and a very tasty Long Man Brewery APA a recommendation for the thirsty train traveller or for those who like a bustling Lewes corner to people-watch.

Chapter Four

Lewes – Southover

22. The Rooks Inn, Southover

Southover really is spoilt for good pubs. If we mention briefly the Rooks Inn, Lewes FC's Harveys-serving bar at their stadium as the first point of call at the eastern end of Southover Street, we can then move onto the King's Head and the Swan, both highlights of a Lewes pub tour.

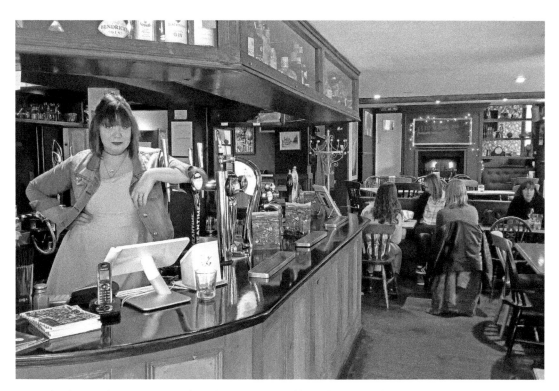

The bar at the King's Head with Kate the landlady firmly in charge.

23. The King's Head, Southover

The King's Head is a true survivor, not only surviving the collapse of owner Enterprise Inns nationwide at the turn of the century, but the year before it opened, Lewes had an incredible sixty-three pubs. The pub was once another Page & Overton house but is now operated by Winsor Ventures, a boutique pub management company who specialise in community pubs and locally sourced food offerings. Their other local pubs include the excellent Foragers in Hove.

It has survived as the King's Head since the current building was built in 1888, with the front bar a public house since at least 1891 when an Emma Goldsmith is named as 'Inn Keeper'. Her family had owned the address for the previous fifty years however, and today the pub is again run by a landlady, with welcoming Australian Kate at the tiller. A building has existed on this corner since at least Tudor times, with previous pubs being called the 'Black Boy' and the 'Chequers'. Although the pub name was used to avoid the displeasure of Henry VIII after the Reformation, the King's Head has used its name only in more recent times. It is however an apt choice as although Henry VIII predates the current pub by centuries, he has greatly affected this area of Lewes, firstly with his order to demolish as much of Lewes Priory as possible, and then giving the house further up the street to his unloved wife Anne of Cleves (the 'Flanders Mare') as part of a generous divorce settlement. Although there is no evidence she ever used it let alone visited it, today the house is called Anne of Cleves House and is a worthy museum. Another king is linked to this area apart from Henry VIII, with William the Conqueror's daughter, Gundrada buried in the nearby one-time priory until her tomb's discovery during Victorian railway tunnelling through the grounds. Gundrada today resides in the nearby Southover Church and for many years it was the King's Head that held the keys to the church, so pilgrims to the tomb were obliged to pop in.

The King's Head is everything a great pub should be. It is cosy but not cramped and has a similar bar layout to the Elly, meaning you feel part of the pub without being supervised. Surprisingly rare for Lewes, it actually has a delightful pub garden proudly boasting views of Lewes castle. A recent refurbishment meant the much-needed disappearance of the former swirling 1980s carpets to restore beautiful wooden floors and the low ceilings. The property has been extended over the years and now encompasses two former cottages that were built with the original row in the 1850s.

The King's has not only got its layout and management right, but its food too. Management describe themselves as first and foremost a 'boozer that is enthusiastic about food'. But the enthusiasm has paid dividends as this was the only Lewes pub to be featured in the 2012 *Good Food Guide*, which championed the pub, saying how 'Traditional wooden floors and low ceilings belie a thoroughly modern culinary approach that does full justice to free-range, seasonal and sustainable produce ... pure flavours are allowed to shine in the starter of the wild rabbit rillettes ... unctuous pot-roasted belly of pork, succulent skirt steak ... exemplary hazelnut tart'.

Tripadvisor also rates the King's highly as their top reviewed pub in the area. Other reviews include: 'Best place 2 dine in Sussex', 'Great pub, amazing service, beautiful beer garden, food to die for, 10/10', 'Exceptional food in beautiful setting', 'Not enough superlatives to describe the place' and 'Best pub food this year'. None other than Olly Smith, TV presenter of *Iron Chef*, even referred to the King's Head as one of his favourite pubs. Even with only two pubs on the old High Street, Southover could very well become the foodie area of Lewes, and it is possible to envisage more pubs or restaurants opening here. For me, however, the King's food was not its most desired feature on a cold spring night when writing this book (and when about to spend the night in an icy campervan), this writer found its malt whiskies and roaring fire kept him warm and happy and able to postpone his arctic resting place!

24. The Swan Inn, Southover High Street

The Swan, after its construction in around 1750 would have been the first Lewes pub that weary travellers would have seen returning on the coastal road from Seaford Bay. This might be why it was one of the pubs used by smugglers, its customers even once having their contraband confiscated. It is the third pub to hold this name in Lewes, renamed from its original name of the Bell (after Bell Lane, which it sits on the corner of) and after another Swan, also in Southover and also closed down. This is not to be confused with the Swan in Malling Street, Cliffe, which was still open until 1919 and is now an antiques emporium. Quite why the Bell preferred another Southover pub's name is a mystery – possibly the landlord had run the older Swan or was attempting to bring that pub's clientele across. It has been a Verrall's pub and is today part of the Harveys empire.

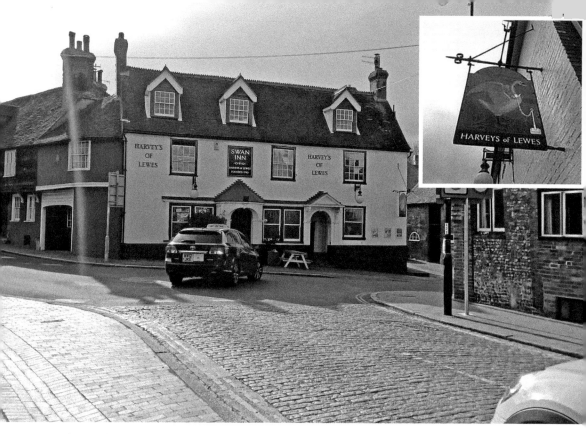

Above: The Swan, a deceptively busy pub in a quiet street.

Below: The bar at the Swan: the place to access good food, good beer and good vinyl.
Inset: The Swan's sign.

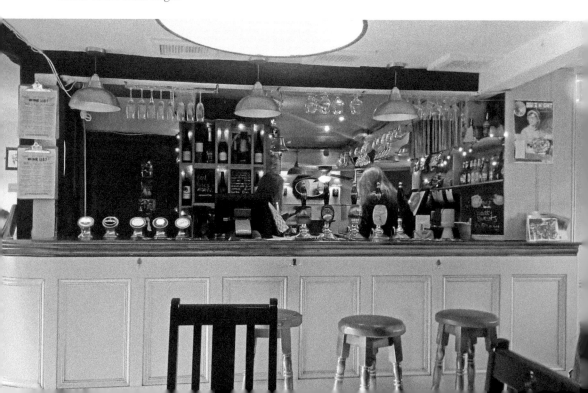

Today the Swan has one of the liveliest Saturday crowds experienced anywhere on a Saturday afternoon across Lewes, helped by an entertaining music venue in the pub's right-hand bar. It is one of those pubs where you want to sit in different places as they all look like your favourite spot, eat everything on the menu and try every beer. The food is, like the King's Head, excellent and the venison burgers are not to be missed. The greatest thing about the Swan though is its vinyl-only music policy. It is a great combination of a youthful pub in a historic building. Southover Street may have its usual ability to seem like a ghost street at times, but the Swan is always full of life and liveliness.

Chapter Five

Lewes Area

25. The Juggs, Wellgreen Lane, Kingston

Moving outside Lewes to visit a selection of nearby pubs, we head south from the Swan to the village of Kingston, where we come to the Juggs, which has a massive beer garden; on first impressions the bar itself appears tiny, but wonderful. Originally one of the village houses, the

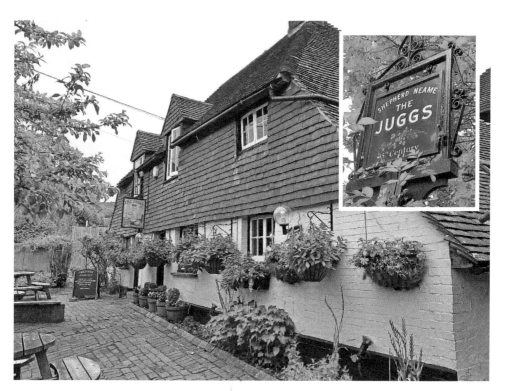

The Juggs, 2016. *Inset*: The Juggs pub sign.

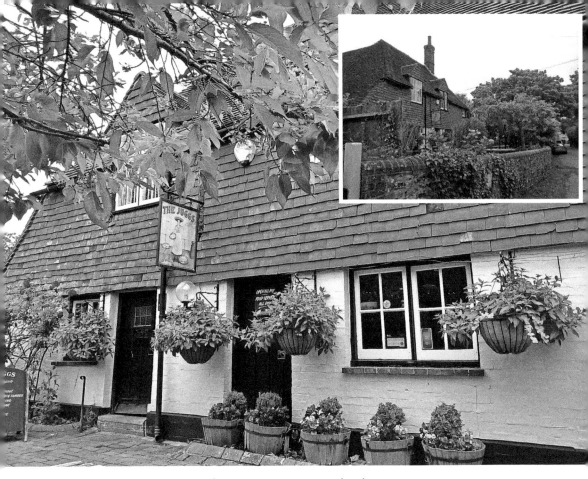

The Juggs in bloom. *Inset*: The Juggs is a more rural pub.

Juggs is one of the later additions to the Lewes district pub scene but has made up for it with its delightful village location, pretty pub gardens and use of such a gorgeous tiled Downland building. It takes its name from the lane it is in, which takes its name from the lane that fishermen would bring 'juggs' of fish up from the coast. Without the Juggs, Kingston wouldn't have as much charm as it does as a village. Like the Ram, which is further east at Firle, it is just five minutes' walk from the foot of the South Downs and a good place for exploring them. This makes both these pubs two of Sussex's finest rural pubs and explains their constant ebb and flow of customers.

It is an intimate occasion inside the Juggs, and even this author who is 5-foot-notverymuch has to almost duck under the original oak beams. Being so cosy, it means you are very lucky to get seats near the log fire in winter, and it can get very crowded, so thankfully once you get past the small front bar there is another bar area and two restaurant rooms, but in summer there is no better reason to choose to eat outside. There's a large car park and a kids' playground (council owned) near the pub and as it is pet and family friendly, it will always be a lively pub full of noise and laughter in the summer months and even has a heated outdoor area for when the great British summer lets us down (as it inevitably does).

Despite being a Shepherd Neame's pub, Harveys Sussex Best is also ever present. On the food front, the Juggs has the usual service of offering take away fish and chips during food service hours. It is a quieter pub than another outer-Lewes pub, the Trevor, in terms of its range of activities offered but still has a quiz night, usually held on the last Wednesday of the month.

26. The Ram Inn, Firle

Our route takes us east now but if we were travelling from Lewes to Firle it is still possible to take a short cut out of Lewes on foot or by car through the industrial estate south of Cliffe and drive through Southerham. Southerham may not feel much like a village these days, surrounded by busy roads and hemmed in against the Downs behind, but when the village had its own inn, the Fox, it must have felt more of a community. The Ram Inn at Firle is certainly part of a community, a vibrant farming community and estate, and definitely helps make Firle what it is. It has been the heart of the village for over 500 years, one of four inns that once existed in this pretty village, recently voted in the top ten places to live in the South East by the *Sunday Times* (Chichester and Midhurst were the other two Sussex mentions). The other pubs were the Woolpack, the Beanstalk and the wonderfully named Polecat. The oldest record of a hostelry in evidence seems to be an alehouse run by William Ockenden, back in 1641, but it is unclear which, if any of the four above this was, or whether the pub had a fifth tavern.

The village, which was technically West Firle until 1974 and some say still is, despite there being no need for the added prefix as there is no other Firle, East or otherwise. It has been recorded as 'Furle' at one point, though. It is happily perched at the foot of the Downs and is in the South Downs National Park. The rambling old building has three main bar areas, each with its own open fire lit every day between October and April. You may be lucky enough to bump into a range of

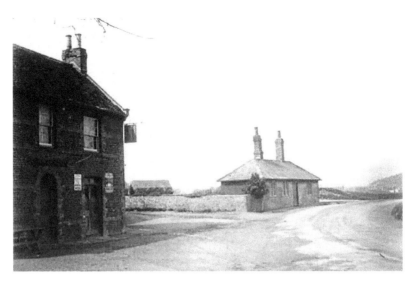

The Fox at Southerham – long since gone, but on the old route once taken to the Ram.

artists, walkers, writers, farmers, farriers and vicars, and the garden is usually full of families and children of all ages. After experiencing its amazing range of food and cask ales, you can now choose to stay at the Ram in one of their four beautiful bedrooms.

On the subject of accommodation, the Ram experienced Canadian soldiers billeted in the pub during the Second World War where, unlike one Lewes pub, they seem to have mixed well with the locals. The only downside it seems to the residency of our cousins from the North American dominion was that the tradition of the Friday night singalongs died out. Prior to the war, locals would take turns to sing. Thankfully, this was resurrected after the war when landlady Mary Hufflett and her husband George brought the tradition back – and ever since it has continued, but on a Monday.

This is about the biggest change that the Ram has probably experienced this century. Firle has been protected from change for centuries by the local landowning Gage family and also by being in a quiet backwater and dead-end off the main A27. You really do feel here more than anywhere that you are deep within the South Downs National Park. A trip to the Ram can be a day out by itself as in between food, drinks and bed you can explore one of Sussex's best-preserved rural villages and the best of our county's countryside.

What I love about Firle, as the Ram's website says, is that 'the main street peters out at the top of the village where the downs begin to rise more steeply and this, along with the lack of through traffic, street lights and road markings give the village a timeless quality'. The village has resisted most development as it is near impossible to buy a property in the village and the householders mostly rent from the Gage Family of Firle Place.

The Ram is an ideal starting point for exploring Firle as it sits at the centre of the village and an easy stroll from Firle Place, the cricket ground, village post office and St Peter's Church. As you explore you really do appreciate the beauty of the village and understand just why the surrounding countryside has attracted artists and writers for generations. Another attraction is Firle's Burning Sky microbrewery which is growing in reputation. It is good to see brewing back as part of the life of Firle because the pub was once important for brewing beer for the Gage's Firle Estate and its workers.

The pub was also important in the village's history for other reasons. The earliest map showing the Ram is from 1775, although, like a number of Lewes pubs, there have been people living in the building since the sixteenth century, which is when the rear bar dates from. The name of the Ram comes from the crest of the Gage family, owners of the Firle Estate and remarkable survivors as former Catholic gentry at the time of the Reformation, Elizabethan England and the Civil War when this part of the county was mostly for Parliament.

The Ram was once a dairy as well as a brewery, which might explain the need for more rooms when it was extended to its current layout (except for the flat-roofed extension to the main bar) sometime between 1770 and 1793. The last extension was added between 1899 and 1910 and since then the Ram has seen little change, except for removal of internal walls to make the bars bigger in 1959 and a short closure for a revamp in 2005. It has been the Ram since sometime just before 1775, when it was known as 'Teeling's House' after its owner. Whether Teeling ran an alehouse is not clear.

Moving on to the 1800s, in 1818 Henry Mockett took over the pub and it stayed in his family for four generations. Mockett seems to have done well in the brewing and pub-running trade, as he left £800 in his will, a decent-sized amount for that time. The Haffendens, with a rare old Sussex surname, were another long-serving family who passed the pub down the generations. They ran the Ram from 1901–85, starting with the first of the Haffendens, Stephen.

One other long-lasting inhabitant, according to Georgia Wells, the current manager and Hayley Bayes, the owner, is Peggity the in-house ghost. She sounds the most exciting of all the Lewes ghosts. In tune with the pub's musical past and fame today (legendary band Squeeze has played on the 'Beach' outside), Peggity makes a spooky tune by tapping her wooden leg. She does this in the old courtroom area of the pub, today the restaurant. Peggity is said to be a young basket maker who was apparently found dead in the pub attic. It is surprising that the courthouse of this one-time coaching inn doesn't have more criminal spirits looming as many of them were sentenced from this room.

From wrongdoers to the righteous, a regular visitor is the local vicar, Peter Owen Jones. He has been found on many BBC productions. Any BBC sitcom about a village pub would no doubt have a butler as a regular, and the real-life Ram has just that. Firle Place's butler frequents the Ram daily for his pint of Harveys Best. Bill Murray of *Ghostbusters* and *Lost in Translation* fame also once popped in. Whether or not he was filmed drinking whisky has not been established.

27. The Cricketers, Berwick Village (off A27 to Eastbourne)

This is as far away from Lewes to the east as we travel and is really nearer to Alfriston than Lewes but the Cricketers merits inclusion due to the amazing views it offers, its wonderful, tranquil cottage gardens and the dreamy interior that will remind frequenters of the Juggs of their local. Who can resist a traditional flint-stone cottage pub nestling below the South Downs? Anyone exploring this far east from Lewes on foot will need to try the Cricketer's home-made food using local produce and it is good to see here that though we have left the surroundings of Lewes you still get Harveys ales here served direct from the cask.

The Cricketers is popular with walkers as it is located near the South Downs Way in Berwick, between Lewes and Eastbourne, which is good as you can return to Lewes now by train or even stop at the tiny station at Glynde for a visit to the Trevor.

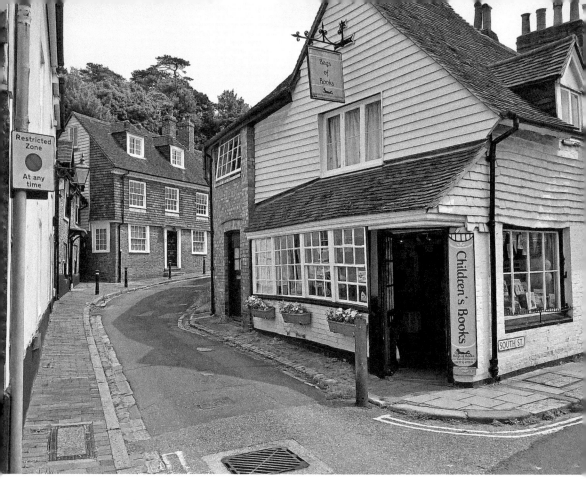

Chapel Hill, the street that housed Cliffe's long-lost Cricketers pub, and a wonderful way to walk from Lewes to the Cricketers in Berwick, the Ram Inn and the Trevor.

28. The Trevor, Glynde

By now anyone using this book for a day or series of day walks from Lewes will be in need of a good rest after their long walk, and the Trevor is a great place to do this. It has Mount Caburn as your backdrop while you spend time enjoying the pub's truly extensive beer garden. The Trevor may not be in the middle of Lewes but it always seems busy when I visit and this may be down to its hectic programme of events including beer festivals, pie nights, fish and chip evenings, folk and live music nights and scooter rallies, all of which are regular events. Not many pubs boast that you can watch paragliders launching themselves from the top of Mount Caburn while families have a Sunday lunch and the children play in the pub's little playhouse or feed the chickens. It may be a train ride out of Lewes but the Trevor takes the local toads' league games very seriously.

Glynde village is lucky to have this free house specialising in regularly changing local cask ales and world beers by the bottle. The pub was built in 1865 by John Harvey of Harveys Brewery in Lewes. The land was owned by Henry Trevor, owner of Glynde Estate and the pub is named after him. The current owners bought the pub from Harveys in 2011 and although it is now a free house, they always have at least one cask of Harveys on tap for those who feel they cannot miss their favourite tipple.

In cooler months, wood burners blaze away in each of the cosy rooms.

29. The Anchor Inn, Barcombe

We don't have enough room in this book to feature all of the truly wonderful country pubs in this lovely and mostly unspoilt parts of rural Sussex. However, I hope that I make up for this by the fact that I've left no better place to end our tour of Lewes and Lewes area pubs than the Anchor, which has now moved outside the town in a northerly direction to the west bank of the River Ouse, 4 miles upstream from the county town. Built in 1790, the Anchor may seem a strange name for pub 11 miles inland, but then makes sense when you realise the Ouse was once much wider and navigable all the way up to the Balcombe Viaduct (which was built with bricks transported up that river). Our waterside end to our very long pub crawl leads us to a pub that has a long history, and today offers two cosy bars and two restaurant rooms, but also boats that can be hired to explore the surrounding countryside. There are also rooms and a marquee available for any type of wedding, event or function. The Anchor Inn is licensed to hold civil wedding ceremonies. This means that we end up not just at a pub, but a well-kept secret that takes some finding without a satnav (especially if you mistake Balcombe for Barcombe as many do). It is also, as I mentioned earlier, a reminder of just how splendid a real riverside pub can be, especially on a hot summer's day. It is a clarion call for Lewes entrepreneurs to wake up and realise the town needs its own truly riverside establishment. A new 'Bear' should be the goal of the business community, providing a waterside world of wonderful memories and moments. How wonderful to have a pub you can reach by boat.

So, why not end our enjoyable journey through the pubs of Lewes district with a boat trip and then a pint at the river's edge? Even more wonderfully, you will be sitting by or on the river that long ago

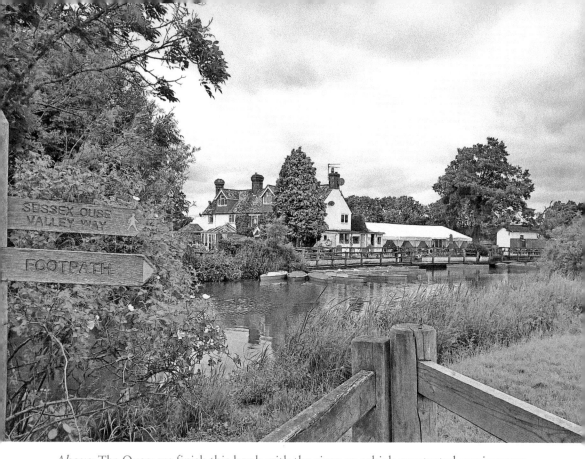

Above: The Ouse: we finish this book with the river on which we started our journey.

Below: The Anchor Inn, 2016.

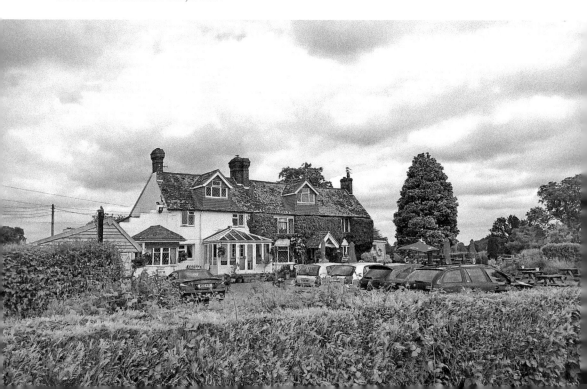

carved out the Ouse Valley and shaped the wonderful town of Lewes. Without the Ouse, there wouldn't have been a need to build the first crossing of the river upstream from the sea that the town developed around. Without the river, there would have been no gap in the downs that made and makes Lewes a place travellers by land or water had to pass through for countless centuries. Without the river, King Alfred wouldn't have an easily defended site to build his waterside burh to protect the area from further Viking attacks. Nor would the Normans have chosen to build their castle to prevent further invaders and control the local Saxons living nearby. We started this book by the Ouse, that lifeblood of Lewes, at the Snowdrop, and we now end further upstream, looking at the water that half an hour or so later will be flowing past the Snowdrop after travelling through the gorgeous and charismatic town that is Lewes.

I'd like to leave the last words to Kathy Simmonds, landlady and one of the second generation in her family of owners of the Brewers Arms. She is spot on when she says it is incredibly hard to explain what makes a pub special; essentially it's the people in it. Even more importantly she raised the point I'd like to finish with: 'Lewes is blessed with the number and variety of its pubs, but they will only survive if people use them. Pubs are valuable community assets.' Kathy is correct, pubs are more than just a place to eat or drink. They are not even just about alcohol these days; families and coffee drinkers are just as important as a stream of revenue. I quoted Belloc, that Sussex patriot, at the start of the book who warned of losing our pubs as we will have lost the last of England. When we lose them we will perhaps have lost the best of England, too.

Acknowledgements

Many thanks to Alan Murphy at Amberley for commissioning this book and Clare, Becky and all the team there for all of their support.

There are many thanks I need to make for all the time that Lewes publicans, hotel and bar staff and Lewesians in general kindly gave up to help me create this work.

Special thanks goes to the Ram Inn for their understanding when our planned visit was suddenly curtailed.

Marion Smith was especially helpful in providing evidence on the lost Crimean Inn and Huw at the Elly was most helpful. Dave and the regulars/residents at the Crown nearly ruined a day's research by being so welcoming and ensuring no other pubs were visited one Saturday by their provision of food, a rare tour and the Grand National on the telly. Gabi Stern at the Snowdrop dropped everything (pardon the low-quality joke) to get me Snowdrop photos at short notice.

My wonderful wife, Laura, has been responsible for the best photos in this book not attributed to other sources. She tirelessly made regular journeys to and from Lewes trying to achieve the impossible and get a sunny half hour for photos during early summer 2016.

Mike Gilson, passionate advocate of all things Sussex, graciously allowed me access to the *Argus*'s archives and images, which helped greatly.

Marc Scruby of Lewes Priory School deserves a mention for kindly affording me the unusual offer of overnight hospitality that his school could provide.

The Tourist Information Centre on the High Street is a rare gem, with my thanks to Tim, Debby and the staff there.

Kathy and all the staff and regulars at the Brewers who supported my research in a huge group effort definitely deserve my thanks.

Thanks also to Laura, Lee and Terry for their willingness to accompany me on the arduous task of visiting and revisiting Lewes pubs in researching this book and my parents for looking after the weapons of mass destruction that are my two sons so we could 'research/drink much Lewes beer' (delete as applicable).

I hope readers have as much fun trying out the route I have suggested as I have had researching and writing it – don't do it all at once, though. Much better to leave that for people like Freddie Flintoff.

Further Reading:

History Trail of Lewes, Edna and Mac McCarthy, SB Publications.
Our Lewes, David Arscott, Sutton Publishing, 2004.
Lewes, Alec Clifton-Taylor, The Alistair Press, 1990.
The Chronicles of The Cliffe and South Malling 688–2003 AD, Brigid Chapman, Book Guild, 2003.
A History of The Ram Inn at Firle, Andrew Lusted, 2007.
Mark Steel's In Town, Mark Steel, Fourth Estate, 2011.
Lewes Then And Now, Bill Young/David Arscott, SB Publications, 2004.
The Lewes Flood, Andy Thomas, SB Publications, 2001.
Lost Lewes, Kim Clark, SB Publications, 2002.
The Inns of Lewes Past and Present, Davey & Whitehall, Pomegranate Press, 2006.
The Pubs of Lewes, East Sussex 1550–2000, David and Lynda Russell, Lynda Russell Publishing, 2015.
Past copies of the *Sussex Express* and *Argus*.